WHO IS JESUS?

WHO IS JESUS?

DEEP TRUTHS OF THE BIBLE
REVEALED IN SMALL GROUP BIBLE STUDIES

JOHN MICHAEL BLAIR

WESTBOW
PRESS
A DIVISION OF THOMAS NELSON

WestBow Press books may be ordered through booksellers or by contacting:

WestBow Press
A Division of Thomas Nelson
1663 Liberty Drive
Bloomington, IN 47403
www.westbowpress.com
1-(866) 928-1240

WestBow Press books may be purchased in bulk for educational, business, fund-raising, or sales promotional use. For more information, call 1.866.928.1240 x1

Because of the dynamic nature of the Internet, any web addresses or links contained in this book may have changed since publication and may no longer be valid. The views expressed in this work are solely those of the author and do not necessarily reflect the views of the publisher, and the publisher hereby disclaims any responsibility for them.

Certain stock imagery © Thinkstock.
Any people depicted in stock imagery provided by Thinkstock are models, and such images are being used for illustrative purposes only.

ISBN: 978-1-4497-3055-0 (sc)
ISBN: 978-1-4497-3056-7 (hc)
ISBN: 978-1-4497-3054-3 (e)

Library of Congress Control Number: 2011919650

Printed in the United States of America

WestBow Press rev. date: 11/14/2011

To Shelly, my best friend,
partner in life and true love.

Table of Contents

Preface

The content of this book is designed for Sunday school classes and small-group Bible studies in homes. The purpose of this book is to give the Sunday school teacher or small-group facilitator the necessary tools and information to lead effective, engaging, and interesting discussions with minimal research and preparation. This is the research and the prep.

The material in this book is presented as a series of thought-provoking questions that generate interesting discussions and lead participants to revelations and new perspectives that change hearts and lives. Seekers will be taught, challenged, and nurtured in their journey. Christians will be fed and enlightened with an understanding of the deeper truths of the Bible.

Because faithful and sincere Christians disagree on many doctrinal issues, this material strives to be fair and present the main arguments from the most prominent sides of an issue. None of the arguments presented are intended to be in-depth analyses or change anyone's thinking. The presentation of differing points of view is merely to make the teacher or facilitator aware of possible issues that could arise in a group discussion.

SUNDAY SCHOOL CLASSES

After 30 years of teaching classes, experience shows that audiences love discussions and hate lectures. This material will help teachers ask the right questions to generate dynamic discussions that teach and feed.

SMALL-GROUP BIBLE STUDIES

Since the beginning of the church, Christians have gathered in small groups to study God's Word. The effectiveness of these small-group Bible studies can be seen in the example of the Paul's small group discussions in the School of Tyrannus (Acts 19:9-10). In just two years, "all those who lived in Asia heard the word of the Lord Jesus."

Today, the widespread use of similar, discussion-oriented Bible studies testifies to their benefit and potential. Some Christians use these small-group discussions as tools for evangelism. Others have found that they present excellent fellowship opportunities. This discussion guide helps small-group leaders or facilitators create an environment that builds fellowship and changes lives.

Introduction

The format of this study guide is designed to promote interesting and engaging discussions. The approach is question and answer rather than lecture. Discussions, when facilitated properly, are a process of discovery far more powerful than listening to a lecture. This guide presents known biblical scholarship in a way that causes participants to wrestle with concepts and forge new perspectives. In fact, some of the most powerful lessons contained in this study focus on how old perspectives (old wine bags) can limit understanding (new wine).

The approach for the study guide is to break each chapter into logical sections that can be read and discussed. The intent is for someone in the group to read a section (e.g., Mark 1:1-8) and for the group leader or facilitator to ask questions to generate discussion.

ASK THE RIGHT QUESTIONS

Anyone can read a passage of scripture and ask questions. Bad questions kill discussions. Good questions lead to good discussions. Effective discussions occur if the questions help the participants discover the true message of the text and relate that message to their daily lives. Questions that are too obvious, too obscure, or too irrelevant kill discussion. Interesting and effective discussions develop when the questions motivate discovery and help participants understand new meanings.

This book provides valuable, time-tested questions that generate the right discussions. This book also provides thorough answers to the questions. The thorough answers are not intended to be read. The answers are intended to give the facilitator an understanding of how to lead the discussion and what points could be made. **Do not ask every question. Choose the questions and information you think are most relevant to your class or discussion group. Do not try to cover every point in the answers. Trying to state all the information in the answers will turn the discussion into a lecture.** Ask questions. Supply relevant historical information from these answers when necessary. Listen to what participants say.

These questions have been used with countless classes and small groups for over 30 years. Each successive group sharpened the quality of the questions and the accuracy of the study by contributing information and insight. The result is a study guide that combines biblical scholarship, practical insights, and powerful group dynamics to create a life-changing environment. Of course, the topic of this study guide, "Who is Jesus?" is the most life-changing subject imaginable.

HELPFUL REMARKS

The subject of this study guide is the identity of Jesus Christ as presented in the gospels, the first four books of the New Testament. Mark is the shortest of the gospels, with 16 chapters, and forms the basis of this study. Passages from the other gospels, as well as the entire Bible, are referenced, included, and reviewed when appropriate.

The Gospel of Mark, as well as the whole Bible, is fully inspired by God. Whenever this study guide refers to Mark as the author of a passage, it is a reference with full knowledge that God is the true author.

Every passage of scripture has both a literary and historical context. Taking a passage out of either context allows its meaning to be twisted and distorted.

There is an old sermon illustration that tells of a man who decided to open the Bible, point to a scripture and do whatever it said. He opened his Bible to Matthew 27:5b. Talking about Judas, it said, "He went away and hanged himself." Thinking that could not be right, he decided to try again. He opened his Bible and pointed to Luke 10:37b, "Go and do likewise."

The meaning of any passage of scripture can be twisted and distorted if it is taken out of its literary and historical context. It is critically important to keep a passage of scripture in its context. God used human authors to deliver His messages to intended recipients. We have to ask ourselves what the original author was trying to say to the original audience. If modern readers conclude that a passage of scripture means *X* but the original audience could not possibly accept or understand *X*, then we do not have the true meaning of the passage. Once we understand what was said to the original recipients and why, we can accurately apply it to our lives today.

As an example, people read the story about the feeding of the 5,000 and conclude that we should feed the hungry. While feeding the hungry is critically important, the point of the story has very little to do with feeding hungry people. It is primarily concerned with taking responsibility for your actions and illustrates that the twelve disciples completely misunderstood what Jesus was doing. Understanding what a passage meant to the first century recipients allows us to accurately understand what it means to us today.

This guide provides enough historical information to allow the group to understand the historical context of Jesus and his message. The discussion questions continually establish both contexts (literary and historical) by emphasizing the structure of the material and the historical, first-century background.

WHICH BIBLE TO USE

Many people like the New American Standard Version of the Bible. Others like the wording in the New International Version. Others like more modern sounding translations or paraphrases. It seems preferences are based largely on how people put sentences together (syntax) and understand meaning.

There are also a few people who cling to the King James Version of the Bible as the only true Bible. They reason that if it was good enough for the apostle Paul, it is good enough for them. To each his own.

In classes and group Bible studies, it is often enriching to hear various translations of the Bible. The biggest disadvantage to having various translations in a group study is that sometimes participants have a hard time following a reading when the passage is worded in different ways.

The translation of the scriptures used here is the World English Bible. This is an accurate and reliable translation and allows free distribution and use without copyright and licensing issues (public domain). The description on the website for the translation states, "The World English Bible is based on the American Standard Version of the Holy Bible first published in 1901, the Biblia Hebraica Stutgartensa Old Testament, and the Greek Majority Text New Testament." More information is available at http://ebible.org. You can download the entire Bible for free at http://ebible.org.

Background
of the Book of Mark

Authorship

The Gospel of Mark does not specify an author. The early church believed Mark was the author. Eusebius, writing in the early fourth century A.D., quoted Papias from A.D. 140 saying, "And John the Presbyter also said this, Mark being the interpreter of Peter, whatsoever he recorded he wrote with great accuracy . . . He was in company with Peter, who gave him such instruction as was necessary."[1]

Irenaeus, writing around A.D. 185, said, "Mark, the disciple and interpreter of Peter, also transmitted to us in writing what had been preached by Peter."[2]

Eusebius quoted Clement of Alexandria from about A.D. 200, saying, "When Peter had proclaimed the word publicly at Rome, and declared the Gospel under the influence of the Spirit; as there was a great number present, they requested Mark . . . to reduce these things to writing, and that after composing the Gospel he gave it to those who requested it of

---

[1]   Eusebius, *Ecclesiastical History*, (A.D. 325), 3:39:15
[2]   Irenaeus, *Against Heresies*, (A.D. 180), 3·1·1

him. Which when Peter understood, he directly neither hindered nor encouraged it."[3]

The second-century writings quoted above show that early church writers held that Mark was closely associated with Peter. This is consistent with 1 Peter 5:13, where Peter refers to Mark as his son. This association probably explains why Peter appears as the main character among the disciples throughout the book of Mark.

Mark is also mentioned several times in the New Testament. In Acts 12:12, Mark was living in Jerusalem with his mother. It seems their home was a center for Christian activity in Jerusalem.

Mark was also related to Barnabas. He began traveling with Paul and Barnabas in Acts 12:25 and went on the missionary journey beginning in Acts 13:1-3. Mark left Paul and Barnabas in Acts 13:13 and returned to Jerusalem. Acts 15:36-41 also recounts a discussion between Paul and Barnabas over Mark. Their disagreement was significant enough to cause them to work separately.

But Mark was not abandoned by Paul indefinitely. In Colossians 4:10, Mark was in Rome helping Paul during his imprisonment. This is also substantiated in another prison epistle, Philemon 24, where Paul calls Mark a fellow worker. Finally, when Paul is nearing martyrdom, he writes to Timothy and asks for Mark, saying that Mark is helpful (2 Timothy 4:11).

Mark is well qualified to write the gospel about Jesus Christ, the Son of God. Because of the statement that Mark wrote about what Peter preached in Rome, we might conclude that the handwriting belongs to Mark, but the content may very well be the Gospel of Peter.

DATE

Trusting Clement of Alexandria, the Gospel of Mark was written in Rome before the martyrdom of Peter. The material in this book fits

---

[3]   Eusebius, *Ecclesiastical History*, (A.D. 325), 6:14:1

its origin in Rome and intended Gentile audience (see the section on Audience below). The other important consideration is that over 50 percent of the material in Mark is quoted in the Gospels of Matthew and Luke. The Gospel of Mark would then have to be dated earlier than these, about A.D. 64 or earlier.

AUDIENCE

Following second-century tradition, Mark was written in Rome for Gentiles. This is consistent with certain characteristics of the book. There is no genealogy or infancy narrative that would be important to Jewish audiences concerned about his ancestry and place of birth. There are several explanations of Jewish customs (example: Mark 7:3-4), which would be necessary for Gentile readers but strangely out of place for Jewish readers. Also, Mark included several Latin words, which fit a Roman audience.

PURPOSE

The purpose of the Gospel of Mark is to reveal the identity of Jesus and to declare that Jesus is the Christ, the Son of God. The first eight chapters of Mark's gospel (up to the climactic question in Mark 8:27, "Who do people say I am?") continually raise the question of Jesus' identity. A good example is in Mark 4:41. After Jesus calms the storm, the disciples actually ask the question, "Who is this?" Mark identified Jesus as the Christ, the Son of God.

HISTORICAL SETTING

Jesus was actually born before 4 B.C. (There was a clerical error in setting "the year of our Lord." Under the Julian Calendar, a sixth-century monk, named Dionysius Exiguus, incorrectly calculated Jesus' birth. The Gospel of Matthew states that Jesus was born during the reign of King Herod the Great, who died in 4 B.C.)

Luke 2:1 tells us that Augustus was Caesar at the time of Jesus' birth. Because of a census, Joseph and Mary traveled from Nazareth to

Bethlehem where Jesus was born. These areas were known as Galilee, Judea, and Samaria. The whole region was part of the Roman Empire and under Roman occupation. Roman soldiers maintained control, enforced Roman law, and made sure taxes were collected. Many Jews hated the Romans and there was constant talk of revolution and freedom. Many revolts and uprisings occurred. Barabbas is specifically mentioned as an insurrectionist in Mark 15:7.

Rome allowed the Jews to have a Jewish king that was installed and controlled by Rome. The Jews also had a Sanhedrin that oversaw temple worship and was the religious authority for Judaism. The Sanhedrin, with the Chief Priest as the head, was less controlled by Rome but still bowed down to Rome's authority to keep the Jews from being massacred by the Roman armies (which actually happened around A.D. 70).

According to first-century historian Titus Flavius Josephus[4] there were three main sects of Jews that represented three world perspectives popular among first-century Jewish people. These were the Pharisees, the Sadducees, and the Essenes. There was also a political group known as the Zealots who are sometimes referred to as the fourth sect.

The Pharisees accepted the first five books of the Old Testament (the Torah) as religiously authoritative but also accepted the rest of the Old Testament and the oral tradition of the Jews that defined how to obey the commandments of God. They believed in resurrection of the dead, the existence of angels and spirits, and an after-life (Acts 23:8).

The Sadducees only accepted the Torah as biblically inspired and binding. They rejected the oral traditions of the Jews as mere teachings of men and not authoritative. They did not believe in an after-life or angels and spirits. They focused on the commands of God in the books of Moses (Torah) and were very legalistic in obeying them.

The Essenes were communal and often separatists. They believed the rest of the Jews were apostate for not observing the law according to their interpretation. They strictly followed the Torah, especially in

---

[4]   Titus Flavius Josephus, *Antiquities of the Jews*, book 18

matters of personal righteousness and purity. They practiced immersion in water baptism for ceremonial cleansings. They avoided marriage, claiming celibacy was more pure.

The Zealots were more of a political sect than a religious one. They hated Rome, Roman control of the Jewish nation, and paying taxes to Rome. They lived for the overthrow of Roman occupation in their region. To support their cause, they relied heavily on Old Testament prophecies that sounded like the Messiah would save Israel from Roman occupation and restore Israel.

CONVENTIONS USED

1.   Some scripture references are bold and underlined:

Mark 1:1-8

Any passage of scripture referenced in bold and underlined is meant to be read by the leader, class, or group. Passages of scripture that are not bold and underlined have been included for additional information but are not necessary to read as a group.

2.   Questions to ask the group are numbered and in bold text:

1.   **What do you think are some of the biggest problems people face today?**

Numbered questions follow each underlined, bold scripture reference and refer to the passage of scripture they follow. It is up to the teacher or group leader to review the questions before the class and choose which questions are the most appropriate to generate discussion. It is not necessary to ask all questions. It is necessary to get people talking and sharing. Ask thought-provoking questions.

3.   Notes to the facilitator are in parenthesis and italicized text:

(Note: Expect participants to share things like debt, divorce, cancer, and maybe even death.)

4. Normal text following a bolded question is offered as a possible answer to the question:

Death is the biggest problem people face today.

Normal text following a question is offered as if the leader were speaking. Again, it is up to the facilitator to customize answers for the needs of the group. Much more information is given in the answers than needs to be given to the group. The amount of information supplied in this study guide is intended to give the group leader a high level of preparation and understanding of historical background. The amount of information to actually present is up to the leader. This level of information also prepares the leader for questions that might be asked.

Many group leaders write the passage of scripture in the margin of their Bible underlined, like "Mark 1:1–8." Then, under it in the margin, they write the questions they want to ask in the order they want to ask them, like "1. What do you think are some of the biggest problems people face today?" Concise notes can follow each question to give the leader reminders. This method works far better than referencing a book or separate pieces of paper with notes.

Someone once asked if writing notes in the margin of a Bible was sacrilegious or adding to the Word of God. Scripture is far more than ink on paper as this verse teaches.

Hebrews 4:12.

> [12]For the word of God is living, and active, and sharper than any two-edged sword, and piercing even to the dividing of soul and spirit, of both joints and marrow, and is able to discern the thoughts and intentions of the heart.

You cannot destroy the Word of God by burning a Bible or tearing out a page. It is far easier to add to the Word or God or change the Word of God through false teaching. If good notes in the margin of a Bible improve the accuracy of your teaching, it seems like a wise practice.

Chapter 1

INTRODUCTORY COMMENTS

The topic of our discussion is "Who is Jesus?" The New Testament gives us four books, called the Gospels, that cover the life of Jesus. The Gospel of Mark is the second book in the New Testament and is the shortest of the four gospels. It has 16 chapters. Mark is going to be our main text for discussing the life of Christ, but we will read parts of Matthew, Luke, and John, and even some of the rest of the Bible as needed.

Besides being the shortest of the Gospels, Mark has other characteristics that make it very appropriate for our discussions. First, the purpose of the Gospel of Mark is to answer the question "Who is Jesus?" Over and over, Mark shows us examples of people wrestling with that question. Second, the Gospels of Matthew, Luke, and John have very long sections of teachings. Mark is more about what Jesus did and his identity. Mark includes many of the teachings of Jesus, but Mark likes action. Action is going to keep us engaged. Third, according to Christians writing in the second century, the Gospel of Mark was written by Mark who was with the apostle Peter in Rome. Peter was preaching to the non-Jewish people of Rome (Gentiles) and telling them about Jesus. Mark wrote down what Peter preached, and it is preserved to this day in the Gospel of Mark. So, the handwriting may be from Mark, but the actual descriptions of what happened are from the apostle Peter.

Let's start in the Gospel of Mark, chapter 1. We are going to take small sections.

Mark 1:1-8

¹The beginning of the Good News of Jesus Christ, the Son of God. ²As it is written in the prophets,

> "Behold, I send my messenger before your face,
> who will prepare your way before you.[5]
> ³The voice of one crying in the wilderness,
> 'Make ready the way of the Lord!
> Make his paths straight!'"[6]

⁴John came baptizing[7] in the wilderness and preaching the baptism of repentance for forgiveness of sins. ⁵All the country of Judea and all those of Jerusalem went out to him. They were baptized by him in the Jordan river, confessing their sins. ⁶John was clothed with camel's hair and a leather belt around his waist. He ate locusts and wild honey. ⁷He preached, saying, "After me comes he who is mightier than I, the thong of whose sandals I am not worthy to stoop down and loosen. ⁸I baptized you in[8] water, but he will baptize you in the Holy Spirit."

1. **What do you think are some of the biggest problems people face today?**

(Note: People will answer with debt, divorce, cancer, and maybe even death.)

Death is one of the biggest problems people face today, if not the biggest problem. Christianity is the only major world religion offering an answer for death. Jesus conquered death and was resurrected. Buddha

---

[5] 1:2 Malachi 3:1
[6] 1:3 Isaiah 40:3
[7] 1:4 or, immersing
[8] 1:8 The Greek word (en) translated here as "in" could also be translated as "with" in some contexts.

was not resurrected. Mohamed was not resurrected. In Hinduism, you might be reincarnated but without continuation of consciousness from one life to another, it does not offer a great answer for death. In Shintoism, popular in Japan, you might join your ancestors in some type of spirit form. In Islam, you face a wrathful God who may or may not have mercy on you. In Christianity, the good news is that God loves you, sent His Son Jesus to conquer death and provide a resurrection and eternal life to those who believe. In Christ, death has no power. You can live forever, and Jesus has already purchased forgiveness and mercy so you do not have to face a wrathful God. In the next few weeks, we are going learn about the good news.

2. **Mark 1:1 looks more like a title than an opening statement. Some translations say, "The beginning of the gospel of Jesus Christ, the Son of God." What does "gospel" mean?**

The word gospel literally means "good news." The good news is that death is not the end. Jesus is the answer to death and a host of other problems we face.

3. **Mark starts his story about Jesus by telling us about John the Baptist. If you were going to write down the story of Jesus, how would you begin?**

(Note: Some people will say that they would begin with the miraculous virgin birth. Reinforce that thought by reminding the group that Matthew and Luke thought the very same thing.)

4. **Why do you think Mark left out the virgin birth and started with John the Baptist?**

If Mark was writing what Peter preached to non-Jewish people in Rome, the genealogy of Jesus and the virgin birth would not have had the same meaning to them. Mark's book is about the three-year ministry of Jesus. The ministry of Jesus began when he was baptized by John the Baptist.

5. In verse 6, we are told about John's clothing. He wore a garment of camel's hair and a leather belt around his waist. Why do you think it was important to tell us what he wore?

In 2 Kings 1:5-8, Elijah, one of the greatest prophets of the Old Testament, is described as having a garment of hair with a leather belt around his waist—the same description Mark gives of John the Baptist. Mark opens his story by quoting Malachi 3:1 and Isaiah 40:3, which are two of the Old Testament prophesies that said Elijah was supposed to come back as a sign that the Messiah was coming. When we get further into the study, we are going to read Matthew 11:11-14, where Jesus declared that John the Baptist was, indeed, the fulfillment of the Elijah prophecy.

John the Baptist was a prophet or messenger from God who was supposed to get people ready for the coming of the Messiah. One of the most convincing proofs that all this is true is the fact that prophets foretold the events and they came true. We are going to look at several of these prophecies later in the book.

6. How did John prepare people for the coming of the Messiah?

He preached "a baptism of repentance for the forgiveness of sins." People repented and were baptized by John for the forgiveness of sins. In other words, people turned away from their evil deeds and committed to live righteous lives for God. Then they were baptized as a ceremonial cleansing.

7. Can baptism in water wash your sins away?

This is a major point of disagreement among churches. Many churches today teach that water cannot wash away sin. They teach that baptism is an outward sign of an inward condition. The Bible teaches us in Ephesians 2:8-9 that "⁸for by grace you have been saved through faith, and that not of yourselves; it is the gift of God, ⁹not of works, that no one would boast."

Many Christians believe baptism in water cannot forgive sins because that would be a work, as mentioned in the above verses. Other passages of scripture teach that the purpose of baptism is always to forgive or wash sins away. In Acts 2:38-39, the apostle Peter commanded the people who had come to believe to "repent and be baptized for the forgiveness of their sins." Acts 22:14-16 is the account of Ananias telling the apostle Paul to "arise and be baptized and wash your sins away calling on the name of the Lord."

1 Peter 3:18-22 actually states that baptism saves you. The point of this discussion is not to change anyone's mind about baptism but to point out that baptism is a central theme in Christianity and figures prominently in this story. For more information regarding various interpretations of this topic, see the overview of this debate in Appendix A: Various Beliefs About Baptism.

8. What is the difference between John's baptism and the baptism Jesus would bring?

(Note: There have been endless debates over the topic of baptism. Most Christians believe that the Holy Spirit dwells in the modern Christian in one way or another. Most Christians today believe that one of the main differences between the Old Testament and the New Testament is the Holy Spirit, who helps us live a righteous Christian life. Most Christians believe that the Holy Spirit dwells in the Christian when they come to a saving belief in Jesus Christ. Some Christians believe that there is a baptism of the Holy Spirit. Some believe that this baptism of the Holy Spirit occurs without water and others cite Jesus' baptism in support of water being present at baptism. The following information is not meant to change anyone's perspective but offered as interesting commentary to spur discussion. What is critically important is the point that Christianity is a new covenant based on the Holy Spirit, empowering Christians to live a life of love, which fulfills the Old Testament law.)

John baptized in water, but Jesus would baptize with the Holy Spirit. In

Acts 19:1-5, Paul found some people who had been baptized by John but had not received the Holy Spirit. They were baptized again with Jesus' baptism.

Acts 19:1-5

It happened that, while Apollos was at Corinth, Paul, having passed through the upper country, came to Ephesus, and found certain disciples. [2]He said to them, "Did you receive the Holy Spirit when you believed?"

They said to him, "No, we haven't even heard that there is a Holy Spirit."

[3]He said, "Into what then were you baptized?"

They said, "Into John's baptism."

[4]Paul said, "John indeed baptized with the baptism of repentance, saying to the people that they should believe in the one who would come after him, that is, in Jesus."

[5]When they heard this, they were baptized in the name of the Lord Jesus.

In 1 Corinthians 12:12-13, Paul states, "For we were all baptized by one Spirit into one body . . . and we were all given the one Spirit to drink."

One of the promises God made concerning the New Covenant was:

Ezekiel 36:25-27

[25]I will sprinkle clean water on you, and you shall be clean: from all your filthiness, and from all your idols, will I cleanse you. [26]I will also give you a new heart, and I will put a new spirit within you; and I will take away the stony heart out of your flesh, and I will give you a heart of flesh. [27]I will put my Spirit within you, and cause you to walk in my statutes, and you shall keep my ordinances, and do them.

I will sprinkle clean water on you, and you will be clean; I will cleanse you from all your impurities and from all your idols. I will give you a new heart and put a new spirit in you; I will remove from you your heart of stone and give you a heart of flesh. And I will put my Spirit in you and move you to follow my decrees and be careful to keep my laws.

Jeremiah 31:31-34

[31]Behold, the days come, says the Lord, that I will make a new covenant with the house of Israel, and with the house of Judah: [32]not according to the covenant that I made with their fathers in the day that I took them by the hand to bring them out of the land of Egypt; which my covenant they broke, although I was a husband to them, says the Lord. [33]But this is the covenant that I will make with the house of Israel after those days, says the Lord: I will put my law in their inward parts, and in their heart will I write it; and I will be their God, and they shall be my people: [34]and they shall teach no more every man his neighbor, and every man his brother, saying, Know the Lord; for they shall all know me, from their least to their greatest, says the Lord: for I will forgive their iniquity, and their sin will I remember no more.

It is impossible to accurately understand Christianity without understanding these two passages. Christianity is a new covenant between God and man that is not based on keeping the law. The New Covenant includes the Holy Spirit dwelling within the Christian, which motivates the Christian to live a life of love that does fulfill the Old Law. If you love the people around you, you won't steal from them, cheat them, take advantage of them, or kill them. The Christian living by the Spirit does by nature what the law failed to force us to do under penalty of death.

The baptism of the Holy Spirit is the fulfillment of these and similar prophesies. After the day of Pentecost, when the Holy Spirit was made available to people (Acts 2:1-4), Jesus' baptism was instituted. Having the Holy Spirit dwelling within us moves us to follow God's decrees and keep his commands.

Some may ask, "Is there a baptism of the Holy Spirit and a baptism of water or does Jesus' baptism include water?"

Most Christians believe that the baptism of the Holy Spirit occurs when a person comes to a saving belief in Jesus Christ and has nothing to do with water baptism. Some Christians argue that baptism of the Holy Spirit happens at the same time as water baptism and cite the baptism of Jesus and the teaching of John 3.

John 3:1-5

Now there was a man of the Pharisees named Nicodemus, a ruler of the Jews. [2]The same came to him by night, and said to him, "Rabbi, we know that you are a teacher come from God, for no one can do these signs that you do, unless God is with him."

[3]Jesus answered him, "Most certainly, I tell you, unless one is born anew,[9] he can't see the kingdom of God."

[4]Nicodemus said to him, "How can a man be born when he is old? Can he enter a second time into his mother's womb, and be born?"

[5]Jesus answered, "Most certainly I tell you, unless one is born of water and spirit, he can't enter into the kingdom of God!

This argument states that in John 3:1-5, Jesus declared that a man must be born of the water and the Spirit to enter the kingdom of God. Ephesians 4:4-6 declares that there is only one baptism. If there is a baptism of the Holy Spirit discussed in the Bible and a baptism with water, how can there be only one baptism? These background thoughts on various arguments helps prepare us for the next section.

Mark 1:9-11

[9]It happened in those days, that Jesus came from Nazareth of Galilee, and was baptized by John in the Jordan. [10]Immediately coming up from the water, he saw the heavens parting, and the Spirit

---

[9]   3:3 The word translated "anew" here and in John 3:7 (anothen) also means "again" and "from above."

descending on him like a dove. ¹¹A voice came out of the sky, "You are my beloved Son, in whom I am well pleased."

1. **Verse 4 says that John was preaching the baptism of repentance for forgiveness of sins. Hebrews 4:15 tells us that Jesus was without sin. If he had no sin, why was Jesus baptized?**

Jesus' baptism was the beginning point of his three-year ministry. It communicated that he was fully consecrated to do God's will. In Matthew 3:13-17, Matthew states that Jesus' baptism was to fulfill all righteousness—that is, to fulfill all the righteous requirements of God. One of the requirements that had to be met was the anointing of Jesus.

In 1 Samuel 16:3, David was anointed king. He was anointed by a prophet sent by God, which parallels John the Baptist as a prophet sent by God to anoint Jesus as King.

In Exodus 40:12-16, Aaron was anointed high priest. According to Acts 4:25-27, Jesus was anointed at some point.

2 Corinthians 1:21-22

> ²¹Now he who establishes us with you in Christ, and anointed us, is God; ²²who also sealed us, and gave us the down payment of the Spirit in our hearts.

Paul, in 2 Corinthians, stated that God anoints us (Christians), puts his seal of ownership on us, and puts his Holy Spirit in our hearts.

Again, there are two sides to the debate. Most Christians today believe this happens when we believe. Some Christians argue that our anointing and reception of the Holy Spirit occurs when we are baptized into Christ with water. They cite Acts 2:38-39, John 3:1-5, and 1 Corinthians 12:12-13 as proof texts.

Luke 4:18-19 and Acts 10:37-38 seem to teach that Jesus was anointed with the Holy Spirit and power when John baptized him. The baptism of Jesus and the descent of the dove is a beautiful symbol of Jesus' anointing with the Spirit and power, but many believe these events just happened to be together and the Holy Spirit did not descend on Jesus because he was baptized in water. Jesus' baptism was certainly the beginning point of his three-year ministry. It seems to be the moment when devotion and power combined to begin his three-year ministry.

2. In verse 11, who do you think spoke from heaven and how do you think that made Jesus feel?

There is something about the approval of our fathers that is primal or fundamental to our self-esteem. Fathers who withhold approval from their daughters often cause them to seek male attention in odd and sometimes destructive ways. Fathers who withhold approval from their sons often cause similar harm. People often project their relationship with their earthly fathers on God and think God interacts with them in the same way their earthly fathers interacted with them. If dad was absent, distant, and silent, they tend to see God as absent, distant, and silent.

In this situation, Jesus must have felt very affirmed and very close to God. It is probably no coincidence that one of the worst spiritual battles of Jesus' ministry happens next.

<u>Mark 1:12–13</u>

> [12]Immediately the Spirit drove him out into the wilderness. [13]He was there in the wilderness forty days tempted by Satan. He was with the wild animals; and the angels were serving him.

(Note: Matthew gives additional details that help clarify this event.)

<u>Matthew 3:16–4:11</u>

> [16]Jesus, when he was baptized, went up directly from the water: and behold, the heavens were opened to him. He saw the Spirit of God descending as a dove, and coming on him. [17]Behold, a voice out of the heavens said, "This is my beloved Son, with whom I am well pleased."

[1]Then Jesus was led up by the Spirit into the wilderness to be tempted by the devil. [2]When he had fasted forty days and forty nights, he was hungry afterward. [3]The tempter came and said to him, "If you are the Son of God, command that these stones become bread."

[4]But he answered, "It is written, 'Man shall not live by bread alone, but by every word that proceeds out of the mouth of God.'"[10]

[5]Then the devil took him into the holy city. He set him on the pinnacle of the temple, [6]and said to him, "If you are the Son of God, throw yourself down, for it is written, 'He will put his angels in charge of you.' and,

'On their hands they will bear you up,
so that you don't dash your foot against a stone.'"[11]

[7]Jesus said to him, "Again, it is written, 'You shall not test the Lord, your God.'"[12]

[8]Again, the devil took him to an exceedingly high mountain, and showed him all the kingdoms of the world, and their glory. [9]He said to him, "I will give you all of these things, if you will fall down and worship me."

[10]Then Jesus said to him, "Get behind me,[13] Satan! For it is written, 'You shall worship the Lord your God, and you shall serve him only.'"[14]

[11]Then the devil left him, and behold, angels came and served him.

1. Matthew 4:1 says the Spirit led Jesus into the desert to be tempted by the devil. Why did this have to happen?

---

[10]   4:4, Deuteronomy 8:3
[11]   4:6, Psalm 91:11–12
[12]   4:7, Deuteronomy 6:16
[13]   4:10: TR and NU read "Go away," instead of "Get behind me."
[14]   4:10 Deuteronomy 6:13

In Deuteronomy 8, The Israelites are about to enter the Promised Land after wandering in the desert for forty years. Moses explains why they wandered in the desert for forty years and what they should have learned in the desert.

Deuteronomy 8:1–20.

[1]You shall observe to do all the commandment which I command you this day, that you may live, and multiply, and go in and possess the land which the Lord swore to your fathers. [2]You shall remember all the way which the Lord your God has led you these forty years in the wilderness, that he might humble you, to prove you, to know what was in your heart, whether you would keep his commandments, or not. [3]He humbled you, and allowed you to be hungry, and fed you with manna, which you didn't know, neither did your fathers know; that he might make you know that man does not live by bread only, but man lives by everything that proceeds out of the mouth of the Lord. [4]Your clothing didn't grow old on you, neither did your foot swell, these forty years. [5]You shall consider in your heart that as a man chastens his son, so the Lord your God chastens you. [6]You shall keep the commandments of the Lord your God, to walk in his ways, and to fear him. [7]For the Lord your God brings you into a good land, a land of brooks of water, of springs, and underground water flowing into valleys and hills; [8]a land of wheat and barley, and vines and fig trees and pomegranates; a land of olive trees and honey; [9]a land in which you shall eat bread without scarceness, you shall not lack anything in it; a land whose stones are iron, and out of whose hills you may dig copper. [10]You shall eat and be full, and you shall bless the Lord your God for the good land which he has given you. [11]Beware lest you forget the Lord your God, in not keeping his commandments, and his ordinances, and his statutes, which I command you this day: [12]lest, when you have eaten and are full, and have built goodly houses, and lived therein; [13]and when your herds and your flocks multiply, and your silver and your gold is multiplied, and all that you have is multiplied; [14]then your heart be lifted up, and you forget the Lord your God, who brought you forth out of the land of Egypt, out of the house of bondage; [15]who led you through the great and terrible wilderness, with fiery serpents and scorpions, and thirsty ground

where there was no water; who brought you forth water out of the rock of flint; [16]who fed you in the wilderness with manna, which your fathers didn't know; that he might humble you, and that he might prove you, to do you good at your latter end: [17]and lest you say in your heart, "My power and the might of my hand has gotten me this wealth." [18]But you shall remember the Lord your God, for it is he who gives you power to get wealth; that he may establish his covenant which he swore to your fathers, as at this day.

[19]It shall be, if you shall forget the Lord your God, and walk after other gods, and serve them, and worship them, I testify against you this day that you shall surely perish. [20]As the nations that the Lord makes to perish before you, so you shall perish; because you wouldn't listen to the voice of the Lord your God.

In Deuteronomy 8:1-3, Moses explains that God allowed them to be hungry so he could feed them and they could learn that man does not live by bread alone but by God. In Deuteronomy 8:4-18, Moses explained that an abundance of possessions could cause them to become proud and forget God. In Deuteronomy 8:19-20, Moses warned them about worshipping anything other than God.

These three tests in the desert parallel the temptations of Jesus. The Israelites were in the desert forty years, and Jesus was in the desert forty days. Deuteronomy 8:2 says that God led the Israelites in the desert to find out what was in their hearts to see if they would obey Him. I think Jesus faced the same three temptations in the desert but overcame temptation and proved what was in his heart.

2. **Notice that in Matthew 4:3 and 4:6 Satan tells Jesus, "If you are the Son of God . . ." What was Satan trying to get Jesus to do by using the word "if"?**

Satan wanted Jesus to doubt. God wanted Jesus to trust and believe. One of Satan's greatest weapons is doubt.

3. **What do you doubt?**

4. In the second temptation (Matthew 4:6), Satan begins with "if" to cause doubt but this time quotes scripture. How can someone quoting scripture cause you to sin?

We must study the Bible and understand what it says or false teachers will twist the meaning and lead us astray.

2 Peter 3:14–16

[14]Therefore, beloved, seeing that you look for these things, be diligent to be found in peace, without blemish and blameless in his sight. [15]Regard the patience of our Lord as salvation; even as our beloved brother Paul also, according to the wisdom given to him, wrote to you; [16]as also in all of his letters, speaking in them of these things. In those, there are some things that are hard to understand, which the ignorant and unsettled twist, as they also do to the other Scriptures, to their own destruction.

Matthew 7:15–20

[15]"Beware of false prophets, who come to you in sheep's clothing, but inwardly are ravening wolves. [16]By their fruits you will know them. Do you gather grapes from thorns, or figs from thistles? [17]Even so, every good tree produces good fruit; but the corrupt tree produces evil fruit. [18]A good tree can't produce evil fruit, neither can a corrupt tree produce good fruit. [19]Every tree that doesn't grow good fruit is cut down, and thrown into the fire. [20]Therefore, by their fruits you will know them.

There are many warnings in the Bible about false teachers who look like sheep but are really wolves in sheep's clothing. You know them by their fruit. The best defense against people who twist the meaning of scripture is to know what it says and follow it.

The quote that Satan uses is ironic because he quoted Psalm 91:11. Read Psalm 91:11–13. The very next verse speaks of trampling on the serpent.

5. How did Jesus fight these temptations in the desert, and how can we fight temptation today?

Jesus quoted scripture each time. We can fight temptation in the same way if we know what the Bible says and know what is right and wrong. That is why this study is so important.

6. In the third temptation, Satan showed Jesus all the kingdoms of the world and said he could have them. What does Satan show people today to entice them to sin?

(Note: Participants will say that other people are tempted by this and that but, in many cases, they are really sharing what they struggle with.)

Mark 1:14-15

> ¹⁴Now after John was taken into custody, Jesus came into Galilee, preaching the Good News of the kingdom of God, ¹⁵and saying, "The time is fulfilled, and the kingdom of God is at hand! Repent, and believe in the Good News."

1. Mark tells us that Jesus went into Galilee preaching the good news (the gospel). Then verse 15 gives us a summary of his message. What was the message Jesus was preaching?

The time has come. The kingdom of God is near. Repent and believe the good news.

2. What do you think Jesus meant when he said, "The time has come"?

We are going to discover more about time later in the study.

3. Mark 1:1-15 is all one section. Do you think Mark sat down one day and just started writing whatever came to mind, or do you think he structured his thoughts? Is there a structure?

Our modern culture relies on a specific style of structure to convey ideas. Our style relies on Roman numerals and sub-points

I. **Major point one**

    A.   *Sub-point one*

    B.   *Sub-point two*

II. **Major point two**

    A.   *Sub-point one*

    B.   *Sub-point two*

    C.   *Sub-point three*

Many people in the first century used a structure called chiastic, after the Greek letter "Chi," which looks like an X.

Topic 1
Topic 2
Topic 3

Topic 3
Topic 2
Topic 1

The first fifteen verses of Mark follow this chiastic structure.

John
    Topic 1: Gospel (Verse one declares this is the gospel)
    Topic 2: Desert (John is in the desert/wilderness)
    Topic 3: Baptism (John is baptizing)
Jesus
    Topic 3: Baptism (Jesus is baptized)
    Topic 2: Desert (Jesus goes out into the desert/ wilderness)
    Topic 1: Gospel (Jesus is preaching the gospel)

Paying attention to the structure of the writing is going to help us understand what Mark was trying to say.

Mark 1:16-20

> [16]Passing along by the sea of Galilee, he saw Simon and Andrew the brother of Simon casting a net into the sea, for they were fishermen.

> [17]Jesus said to them, "Come after me, and I will make you into fishers for men."

> [18]Immediately they left their nets, and followed him. [19]Going on a little further from there, he saw James the son of Zebedee, and John, his brother, who were also in the boat mending the nets. [20]Immediately he called them, and they left their father, Zebedee, in the boat with the hired servants, and went after him.

(Note: This passage is the beginning of a section that continues to Mark 3:12. In this section from Mark 1:16 to Mark 3:12, there is the calling of the first followers, the identity of Jesus, and the beginning of the battle between Jesus and the religion of his day.

Mark 3:13-19 tells about Jesus choosing the twelve disciples. This parallels Mark 1:16-20, which is the calling of the first followers. Mark 3:13-19 also describes preaching and casting out demons, which becomes the thematic statement for the section from Mark 3:13-19 to Mark 6:6.

Mark 1:16-20, the calling of the first followers, is the head of a major section, so Mark 3:13-19, the choosing of the Twelve, is also the head of a major section.)

1. **Does it seem strange that grown men with families and businesses would just leave their nets and boats to follow Jesus? Why would they do that?**

(Note: Some participants will say that the disciples heard about Jesus or already knew him. Ask what these disciples might have heard about Jesus. The actual answer to this question is not revealed in this study until chapter 6. Leave the question hanging. Tell the group that the answer will be revealed in chapter 6

and use this to create suspense and expectation. Participants will go home and read chapter 6 and come back next week claiming that the answer is not there. Assure them it is and tell them they do not want to miss that week.)

2. How would you feel if you were one of these people and Jesus walked up to you and said, "Follow me"? The question is not "Would you follow?" The question is "How would you feel?"

For the next several weeks we are going to study the life of Jesus. At some point in the study, Jesus may very well say to you personally, "Come, follow me."

Mark 1:21-34

[21]They went into Capernaum, and immediately on the Sabbath day he entered into the synagogue and taught. [22]They were astonished at his teaching, for he taught them as having authority, and not as the scribes. [23]Immediately there was in their synagogue a man with an unclean spirit, and he cried out, [24]saying, "Ha! What do we have to do with you, Jesus, you Nazarene? Have you come to destroy us? I know you who you are: the Holy One of God!"

[25]Jesus rebuked him, saying, "Be quiet, and come out of him!"

[26]The unclean spirit, convulsing him and crying with a loud voice, came out of him. [27]They were all amazed, so that they questioned among themselves, saying, "What is this? A new teaching? For with authority he commands even the unclean spirits, and they obey him!" [28]The report of him went out immediately everywhere into all the region of Galilee and its surrounding area.

[29]Immediately, when they had come out of the synagogue, they came into the house of Simon and Andrew, with James and John. [30]Now Simon's wife's mother lay sick with a fever, and immediately they told him about her. [31]He came and took her by the hand, and raised her up. The fever left her, and she served them. [32]At evening, when the sun had set, they brought to him all who were sick, and those who were possessed by demons. [33]All the city was gathered together

at the door. [34]He healed many who were sick with various diseases, and cast out many demons. He didn't allow the demons to speak, because they knew him.

1. **What do you think it means when it says, " . . . he taught them as having authority, and not as the scribes"?**

The scribes were teachers of the Old Testament and the principles of Judaism. They taught what the book said and interpreted what it meant for the people. Sometimes scribes disagreed on what the Bible meant and how it should be interpreted. The people were often confused and wondered who to believe. Jesus taught the Bible and the true interpretation and the people could know that what he was saying was right because God confirmed it with miracles.

Also note that Mark has begun a critical contrast that will continue through the rest of the book. Jesus and his teaching is compared and contrasted with the scribes and their teaching. In the book of Mark, the scribes and Pharisees represent the religion of Judaism. This is the beginning point for a battle between Jesus and the religion of his day. Jesus did not bring us a new religion. He brought us something much better, which we will learn about.

2. **In verses 23-26, Jesus casts a demon or unclean spirit out of a man. Do you think there are demons or evil spirits that possess people today?**

(Note: Some will say that they have seen people they are sure were possessed. Others will say that there are people in mental institutions that are actually possessed by demons. Others will say that what is described in the Bible as demon possession was actually mental illness. Others will say that we all are possessed by evil spirits from time to time. For whenever someone is overcome by anger, hatred, envy, jealousy, etc. they are under the influence of an evil spirit and do or say things they would not normal do or say. They claim that the anger was talking.)

3. **Who did the evil/unclean spirit think Jesus was?**

The Holy One of God. In other words, the Messiah prophesied in the Old Testament to come and save Israel.

4. **Why did Jesus tell the evil/unclean spirit to be quiet? The evil spirit was telling the truth about who Jesus was. In verse 34, Mark again made a point to say Jesus would not let them speak because they knew who he was. Why? I thought we were supposed to tell everyone that Jesus is the Son of God. Why prevent them from telling the truth?**

(Note: Participants might say, "Jesus didn't want testimony from an evil source." The actual answer will be revealed in chapter 6.)

Mark 1:35–39

> [35]Early in the morning, while it was still dark, he rose up and went out, and departed into a deserted place, and prayed there. [36]Simon and those who were with him followed after him; [37]and they found him, and told him, "Everyone is looking for you."

> [38]He said to them, "Let's go elsewhere into the next towns, that I may preach there also, because I came out for this reason." [39]He went into their synagogues throughout all Galilee, preaching and casting out demons.

1. **Why do you think Jesus got up to pray while it was still dark?**

To get away from the crowds and get his mind right for the day. As soon as the disciples got up, they went to look for him. In fact, everyone was looking for him.

2. **If Jesus needed solitary time to pray, do you think we need that kind of time? What kinds of activities help you get your mind and attitude right?**

(Note: People will share about daily devotional times of Bible reading and prayer and other things that help them.)

Mark 1:40–45

[40]A leper came to him, begging him, kneeling down to him, and saying to him, "If you want to, you can make me clean."

[41]Being moved with compassion, he stretched out his hand, and touched him, and said to him, "I want to. Be made clean." [42]When he had said this, immediately the leprosy departed from him, and he was made clean. [43]He strictly warned him, and immediately sent him out, [44]and said to him, "See you say nothing to anybody, but go show yourself to the priest, and offer for your cleansing the things which Moses commanded, for a testimony to them."

[45]But he went out, and began to proclaim it much, and to spread about the matter, so that Jesus could no more openly enter into a city, but was outside in desert places: and they came to him from everywhere.

1. **What do we know about the disease of leprosy, especially in the first century?**

Leprosy is a vicious and mildly contagious skin disease that causes nerve damage in the arms, legs, and fingers. It also is characterized by skin legions, disfiguring lumps, and weakness in extremities due to nerve damage. It is caused by a microorganism that is controlled in modern times by antibiotics. In times before antibiotics, it was said that leprosy caused a victim's skin to rot off their bones while they lived.

In biblical times, people who contracted leprosy were quarantined in leper colonies. It was important to remove a leprosy victim to contain the spread of the disease. Culturally, to contract leprosy meant your life was over. You lived as an outcast from society. No one would come close to you and no one would touch you. You were slowly eaten by a microorganism while people ran from you. In Jewish law, a leper was not allowed in public places and if someone with leprosy was to be near other people, they had to bang a pot or make some other loud noise warning people a leper was coming. People would run.

2. **Do you think Jesus could have just said, "Be healed" and the leper would have been healed? Why do you think Jesus reached out and touched the man to heal him?**

Most people ran from this man. It may have been years since anyone touched him. Jesus did not run. The man needed healing but he also needed someone to overcome the boundary and separation and touch him.

3. **If you had been this leper and suffered with such a horrible and incurable disease, how would you have felt when Jesus didn't run from you? How would you have felt when he healed you? When he said go offer the sacrifices described by Moses in the Old Testament, would you have done it?**

If you were cleansed from an incurable disease today (sin), would you do what Jesus said?

4. **Jesus acted to help this man. Can you have compassion without action?**

James 2:15-16

> [15]And if a brother or sister is naked and in lack of daily food, [16]and one of you tells them, "Go in peace, be warmed and filled"; and yet you didn't give them the things the body needs, what good is it?

Good wishes are worthless without actions that help. Good intentions are not enough.

5. **Why did Jesus forbid the leper to tell about what happened?**

(Note: Participants may say that Jesus did not want the crowds to get bigger. This is only part of the answer. The full answer will be discussed in Mark 6.

There is a theme developing in the book of Mark about the religion of men being at odds with Jesus. It is important to note that Jesus was not opposed to the Old Testament law. In this case, Jesus commanded the leper to do what the law required. In the next chapter, Jesus opposed the man-made teachings that had been bound upon the people. Here it is important to point out that Jesus did not oppose the law. Jesus supported the law of God. Jesus opposed the religion of men.)

Chapter 2

Mark 2:1-12

[1]When he entered again into Capernaum after some days, it was heard that he was in the house. [2]Immediately many were gathered together, so that there was no more room, not even around the door; and he spoke the word to them. [3]Four people came, carrying a paralytic to him. [4]When they could not come near to him for the crowd, they removed the roof where he was. When they had broken it up, they let down the mat that the paralytic was lying on. [5]Jesus, seeing their faith, said to the paralytic, "Son, your sins are forgiven you."

[6]But there were some of the scribes sitting there, and reasoning in their hearts, [7]"Why does this man speak blasphemies like that? Who can forgive sins but God alone?"

[8]Immediately Jesus, perceiving in his spirit that they so reasoned within themselves, said to them, "Why do you reason these things in your hearts? [9]Which is easier, to tell the paralytic, 'Your sins are forgiven;' or to say, 'Arise, and take up your bed, and walk?' [10]But that you may know that the Son of Man has authority on earth to forgive sins"—he said to the paralytic—[11]"I tell you, arise, take up your mat, and go to your house."

[12]He arose, and immediately took up the mat, and went out in front of them all; so that they were all amazed, and glorified God, saying, "We never saw anything like this!"

1. **Verse 5 says that Jesus saw their faith. Whose faith did Jesus see?**

He saw the faith of the four men who carried their friend to Jesus.

2. **How do you see faith?**

In actions.

James 2:14–26

[14]What good is it, my brothers, if a man says he has faith, but has no works? Can faith save him? [15]And if a brother or sister is naked and in lack of daily food, [16]and one of you tells them, "Go in peace, be warmed and filled"; and yet you didn't give them the things the body needs, what good is it? [17]Even so faith, if it has no works, is dead in itself. [18]Yes, a man will say, "You have faith, and I have works." Show me your faith without works, and I by my works will show you my faith.

[19]You believe that God is one. You do well. The demons also believe, and shudder. [20]But do you want to know, vain man, that faith apart from works is dead? [21]Wasn't Abraham our father justified by works, in that he offered up Isaac his son on the altar? [22]You see that faith worked with his works, and by works faith was perfected; [23]and the scripture was fulfilled which says, "Abraham believed God, and it was accounted to him as righteousness";[15] and he was called the friend of God. [24]You see then that by works, a man is justified, and not only by faith. [25]In the same way, wasn't Rahab the prostitute also justified by works, in that she received the messengers, and sent them out another way? [26]For as the body apart from the spirit is dead, even so faith apart from works is dead.

(Note: Point out that compassion is not compassion unless there are actions. Faith is not faith unless there are actions.)

---

[15]   2:23, Genesis 15:6

3. **If you were very ill and needed to be healed, would the friends you have now carry you to Jesus? Would they tear a hole in someone's roof? What if you needed to be healed spiritually?**

(Note: This is an opportunity to discuss true friendship and whether we as believers are being true friends to unbelieving friends. It is also an opportunity to talk with unbelievers about whether the people they call friends are really friends.)

4. **Why did Jesus refer to himself as the Son of Man instead of the Son of God?**

Daniel 7:13-14

> [13]I saw in the night visions, and behold, there came with the clouds of the sky one like a son of man, and he came even to the ancient of days, and they brought him near before him. [14]There was given him dominion, and glory, and a kingdom that all the peoples, nations, and languages should serve him: his dominion is an everlasting dominion, which shall not pass away, and his kingdom that which shall not be destroyed.

The term "Son of Man" had a Messianic meaning associated with it. Referring to himself as "the Son of Man" associated him with prophesies in the Old Testament.

5. **Verse 6 talks about some scribes or teachers of the law being there. These are the religious leaders of the day. They studied the Old Testament law as a profession. They were experts in Jewish traditions. In the Gospel of Mark, they represent "man-made religion." We are going to see the confrontations between Jesus and this man-made religion of his day get stronger and stronger until the end of Mark, where religion kills Jesus.**

(Note: The term religion is going to be used to describe those things that are earthly, unspiritual, and rob people of life. Terms like Christianity or spirituality are reserved for religion, which is true, godly, and gives people life.)

6. Why did the scribes/teachers of the law oppose Jesus?

The scribes believed that only God could forgive sins. By claiming to forgive the sins of the paralytic, Jesus was claiming to be on the same level with God. This was blasphemy in Jewish law—unless it is true. The scribes had a concept of God that would not allow them to see who Jesus was. Remember that the main theme in the Gospel of Mark is the identity of Jesus.

7. What was Jesus trying to do, and what was his message?

Jesus was revealing who he was. He said something unexpected to the paralyzed man. Instead of saying, "Be healed," he said, "Son, your sins are forgiven." The scribes reasoned that "you can't forgive this man's sins. Only God can forgive sins." Then Jesus explained that two things were about to happen. There would be forgiving sin and there would be healing. Jesus argued that healing is more difficult to do because you can immediately see whether or not the man is healed. Saying that sins are forgiven is easier to do because no one in the room could see whether or not it actually happened. The logic here is that if you can do the harder thing, then surely you can do the easier thing. So, if Jesus could heal someone, surely he can forgive sins. Jesus revealed that he is God through an exercise in logic and healing.

Mark 2:13-14

> [13]He went out again by the seaside. All the multitude came to him, and he taught them. [14]As he passed by, he saw Levi, the son of Alphaeus, sitting at the tax office, and he said to him, "Follow me." And he arose and followed him.

1. Why would Levi quit his job and follow Jesus?

This is the same question asked when the fishermen left their boats and nets to follow Jesus. The answer will be revealed in Chapter 6.

Tax collectors were Jews who worked for the Roman government collecting taxes from Jews to give to Rome. They were required to collect a certain amount of tax and whatever they could collect above that was their wage. Many Jews considered tax collectors to be traitors and extortionists.

Mark 2:15-17

[15]It happened, that he was reclining at the table in his house, and many tax collectors and sinners sat down with Jesus and his disciples, for there were many, and they followed him. [16]The scribes and the Pharisees, when they saw that he was eating with the sinners and tax collectors, said to his disciples, "Why is it that he eats and drinks with tax collectors and sinners?"

[17]When Jesus heard it, he said to them, "Those who are healthy have no need for a physician, but those who are sick. I came not to call the righteous, but sinners to repentance."

(Note: See the historical background information for important information about Pharisees.)

1. Who is doctor/physician in this statement?

Jesus.

2. Who are the righteous (or more accurately, who thinks they are the righteous)?

The Pharisees.

3. Who are the sick (or thought of as being sick)?

The tax collectors and sinners.

4. Do you think the Pharisees were healthier because of their religion?

No. The Pharisees were sinners just as much as the others. In addition to all the normal sins that plague mankind, they also committed the sins of pride, arrogance, and self-righteousness.

Mark 2:18-22

[18]John's disciples and the Pharisees were fasting, and they came and asked him, "Why do John's disciples and the disciples of the Pharisees fast, but your disciples don't fast?"

[19]Jesus said to them, "Can the groomsmen fast while the bridegroom is with them? As long as they have the bridegroom with them, they can't fast. [20]But the days will come when the bridegroom will be taken away from them, and then will they fast in that day. [21]No one sews a piece of unshrunk cloth on an old garment, or else the patch shrinks and the new tears away from the old, and a worse hole is made. [22]No one puts new wine into old wineskins, or else the new wine will burst the skins, and the wine pours out, and the skins will be destroyed; but they put new wine into fresh wineskins."

1. **The Pharisees created a tradition of fasting. If you wanted to be accepted as righteous, you had to fast. This was not a command of God but a religious tradition of men. What are some modern religious traditions that are not commands of God but are used to judge people?**

2. **In verses 19 and 20, Jesus tells them why his disciples are not fasting. What is he talking about?**

It is as if Jesus is the bridegroom at a party. You do not fast at a party. Jesus is prophesying his death and telling them there will be a time to fast in the future.

3. **Jesus continued his reaction to being judged with a statement about old and new cloth and old and new wine skins. What happens if you wash an old garment with a new patch?**

The old garment has been washed many times and already shrunk. The patch, made from new cloth that has not been washed, shrinks and tears away from the old fabric.

4. **What happens to an old wineskin if you put new wine into it?**

New wine is basically unfermented grape juice. That is why it is called new wine. It has not gone through the fermentation process. If you put new wine in a new wine skin, it ferments and produces gases and stretches the new skin. If you keep putting new wine in an old skin, eventually, the old skin cannot take the fermentation process and bursts.

5. What does new wine in old skins have to do with religious traditions and judgments?

Jesus is bringing a new teaching to Judaism and the world. You cannot put Jesus' new teaching in the old structures of Judaism and expect it to survive. You have to get rid of the old religious structures and start new. Sometimes people are the same way. Sometimes a person has to start new in their thinking and perspective to accept the teachings of Jesus.

Mark 2:23-28

> [23]It happened that he was going on the Sabbath day through the grain fields, and his disciples began, as they went, to pluck the ears of grain. [24]The Pharisees said to him, "Behold, why do they do that which is not lawful on the Sabbath day?"
>
> [25]He said to them, "Did you never read what David did, when he had need, and was hungry—he, and those who were with him? [26]How he entered into God's house when Abiathar was high priest, and ate the show bread, which is not lawful to eat except for the priests, and gave also to those who were with him?" [27]He said to them, "The Sabbath was made for man, not man for the Sabbath. [28]Therefore the Son of Man is lord even of the Sabbath."

1. Jesus and his disciples were picking heads of grain and eating them while they walked. Why did the Pharisees (religion again) think this was unlawful?

The Old Testament law commanded the Jewish people to keep the Sabbath holy and do no work on the Sabbath. The Jewish religious leaders through the centuries created hundreds of human traditions to define what that meant. The Sabbath was from sundown Friday to sundown Saturday. According to the religious leaders, killing a fly on the Sabbath was hunting. In some sects of Judaism today, they turn light switches on before Friday at sunset because to flip a light switch after sundown on Friday would be lighting a fire on the Sabbath. Taking a bath on the Sabbath was outlawed because you might spill some water on the floor and that would be washing the floor.

Someone once asked a rabbi, a Jewish teacher, what to do if their house fell on top of them on the Sabbath. It was against the Jewish tradition to lift anything heavy, so they would be trapped. The rabbi thought and thought. Finally, he said, "I have an answer!" He said, "Pray for a Gentile to come along." (A Gentile is anyone who is not Jewish.)

To the Pharisees, picking heads of grain on the Sabbath was harvesting and, therefore, work.

2. **Jesus answered the accusation of religion by reminding them of someone they accepted. King David was someone the Pharisees admired and accepted. In the Old Testament, King David took some bread that was only lawful for the priests to eat. It is as if Jesus is saying, "You accept King David, and he actually broke a law of God. We are only breaking your traditions, but you accuse us and refuse to accept me."**

3. **What do you think he means when he says, "The Sabbath was made for man, not man for the Sabbath"?**

The Sabbath was created by God as a gift to man so we would not work seven days a week. Man was not created to serve the Sabbath or some religious tradition of men. And, by the way, Jesus is higher than the Sabbath.

Chapter 3

<u>**Mark 3:1-6**</u>

¹He entered again into the synagogue, and there was a man there who had his hand withered. ²They watched him, whether he would heal him on the Sabbath day, that they might accuse him. ³He said to the man who had his hand withered, "Stand up." ⁴He said to them, "Is it lawful on the Sabbath day to do good, or to do harm? To save a life, or to kill?" But they were silent. ⁵When he had looked around at them with anger, being grieved at the hardening of their hearts, he said to the man, "Stretch out your hand." He stretched it out, and his hand was restored as healthy as the other. ⁶The Pharisees went out, and immediately conspired with the Herodians against him, how they might destroy him.

1. Why were the Pharisees and Herodians watching Jesus? Why did they want to accuse him?

The Pharisees saw Jesus as a threat to their power over the people. Jesus taught the people to obey God rather than the traditions of men. Jesus was, therefore, a threat to the interests of the Pharisees.

The Herodians were supporters of King Herod and his dynasty. They were in league with the Romans. Rumors circulated that Jesus might be a king. Jesus was, therefore, also a threat to their interests.

2. Why did Jesus make a show and ask, "Is it lawful on the Sabbath to do good or to do harm? To save life or to kill?"

Jesus is making a point. God did not set up laws to rob people of life. He did not establish a day of rest for his people to prevent their healing. In the religious traditions of the Pharisees, it was more important to keep a man-made law than to heal a man with a withered hand.

In the rituals and traditions of the Pharisees, it was against their religion to heal on the Sabbath because they called it work and, therefore, sin. On the other hand, it was acceptable to their religion to go out and plot how to kill someone. Religion robs people of life and healing and good things. Religion can even plot how to murder.

3. **What are some of the characteristics of religious people in this situation?**

Religious people like to judge and accuse. They had stubborn hearts that refused to see the good. They were hypocrites, saying one thing and doing another.

Through the book of Mark we will see that Jesus did not bring us another religion. Jesus brought us a relationship with God. Having a religion is much different than having a relationship. Those who walk with God find life. Those who legalistically follow a religion are robbed of life.

Mark 3:7-12

[7]Jesus withdrew to the sea with his disciples, and a great multitude followed him from Galilee, from Judea, [8]from Jerusalem, from Idumaea, beyond the Jordan, and those from around Tyre and Sidon. A great multitude, hearing what great things he did, came to him. [9]He spoke to his disciples that a little boat should stay near him because of the crowd, so that they wouldn't press on him. [10]For he had healed many, so that as many as had diseases pressed on him that they might touch him. [11]The unclean spirits, whenever they saw him, fell down before him, and cried, "You are the Son of God!" [12]He sternly warned them that they should not make him known.

1. **As Mark 1:16-20 (the calling of the first followers) was the head of a major section, so Mark 3:13-19 (the choosing of**

the Twelve) is a major section that continues through Mark 6:6. This parallels the sending out of the Twelve in Mark 6:7-13.

This section, Mark 3:7-12, is a summary statement for the section from Mark 1:16-20 to Mark 3:7.

2. **The evil spirits (unclean spirits) seemed to know who Jesus was. Do you think someone can know who Jesus is and still do evil? Why?**

Fundamentally, they are evil. Evil can know the truth and ignore it. People today can know the truth and ignore it. Only by acting on the truth can a person be saved. Faith without deeds is dead.

3. **Some churches today preach that all you have to do to be saved is believe. The evil spirits believed Jesus is the Son of God. Were they saved? Why not?**

The Bible defines saving belief as knowledge, trust, and obedience. Many will die knowing as much as the evil spirits (that Jesus is the Son of God). But if that knowledge never caused a change in behavior, it is useless.

4. **Why did Jesus command the evil spirit to be quiet?**

We will find the answer when we discuss Mark chapter 6. (It is important to continue asking these questions to build interest and suspense.)

Mark 3:13-19

> [13]He went up into the mountain, and called to himself those whom he wanted, and they went to him. [14]He appointed twelve, that they might be with him, and that he might send them out to preach, [15]and to have authority to heal sicknesses and to cast out demons: [16]Simon, to whom he gave the name Peter; [17]James the son of Zebedee; John, the brother of James, and he surnamed them Boanerges, which means, Sons of Thunder; [18]Andrew; Philip; Bartholomew;

Matthew; Thomas; James, the son of Alphaeus; Thaddaeus; Simon the Zealot; [19]and Judas Iscariot, who also betrayed him.

1. Why do you think Jesus chose twelve instead of ten or twenty?

Matthew 19:28 tells us that they were chosen to sit on twelve thrones to judge the twelve tribes of Israel. It is also a manageable number of disciples to teach.

2. Were there only twelve apostles?

The word apostle means one who is sent. Through the common usage in their time and usage in the New Testament writings, the word apostle became closely associated with the twelve disciples. In fact, a new definition with qualifications came into being when the Twelve had to choose a replacement for Judas in Acts 1:15-26. In that instance, the qualification was that a member of the Twelve had to be someone who saw Jesus from his baptism to the crucifixion and witnessed the resurrection of Jesus.

In Acts 14:14, Barnabas and Paul were called apostles. In many of Paul's letters, like 1 and 2 Corinthians, he starts off, "Paul, an apostle of the Lord Jesus . . ." Paul and Barnabas were certainly "ones who were sent," but they were not included in the Twelve Apostles.

3. Verse 15 says they were given authority to heal sicknesses. Is that the same as power?

Some would say that God heals by His power and that the apostles were merely given authority to direct God's power if God deemed it appropriate.

Mark 3:20-21

He came into a house. [20]The multitude came together again, so that they could not so much as eat bread. [21]When his friends heard it, they went out to seize him: for they said, "He is insane."

1. **The New International Version of the Bible says, "when his family heard about it, they went to take charge of him for they said, 'he is out of his mind.'" Family is the correct translation. The editors of the World English Bible could not understand how the family of Jesus could think he was insane, so they opted for a less-accurate translation because of their preconceived ideas. Why did his family think he was insane?**

The actual answer will be revealed in chapter 6.

Mark 3:22-30

> [22]The scribes who came down from Jerusalem said, "He has Beelzebul," and, "By the prince of the demons he casts out the demons."
>
> [23]He summoned them, and said to them in parables, "How can Satan cast out Satan? [24]If a kingdom is divided against itself, that kingdom cannot stand. [25]If a house is divided against itself, that house cannot stand. [26]If Satan has risen up against himself, and is divided, he can't stand, but has an end. [27]But no one can enter into the house of the strong man to plunder, unless he first binds the strong man; and then he will plunder his house. [28]Most certainly I tell you, all sins of the descendants of man will be forgiven, including their blasphemies with which they may blaspheme; [29]but whoever may blaspheme against the Holy Spirit never has forgiveness, but is guilty of an eternal sin"[30]—because they said, "He has an unclean spirit."

1. **Why did the scribes or teachers of the Law come down from Jerusalem to oppose Jesus?**

John 11:45-48 describes exactly why the Pharisees and scribes/teachers of the Law were opposed to Jesus. All the people were running to Jesus, and they were afraid this would cause Rome to see a threat and attack them. The religious leaders came from Jerusalem to discredit Jesus and persuade the people to stop following him.

2. **How did religion try to discredit Jesus?**

They said he was on the same side as the devil. But Jesus used reason and logic to discredit their point. If a nation or kingdom of people is divided and fighting a civil war, it cannot stand. If members of a family or household are divided and fighting each other, that family or "house" cannot stand. The family will be torn apart. Therefore, if Satan is casting out his own demons and there is fighting in his own kingdom, his end has come. It may be that Jesus purposely used the image of a family in disagreement because of Mark 3:21.

3. In verse 27, who is the strong man, and what is the possession that gets carried off?

Satan is the strong man in this metaphor, and the people who were possessed by demons are his possessions. In order for Jesus to cast out the demons and take back the people, he must first subdue the strong man and then he can take the possessions.

4. What is the unpardonable sin?

Blaspheming the Holy Spirit is the unpardonable sin. This passage has caused many Christians to live in fear of having committed the unpardonable sin so it is important to understand exactly what Jesus taught. The religious leaders accused Jesus of working by the power of Satan. Since Jesus cast out demons by the power of the Holy Spirit, the religious leaders were seeing the power of the Holy Spirit as evil. The religious leaders were so blinded by their preconceived ideas that they saw good as evil. How could someone so twisted ever come to God for forgiveness? The point is that anyone who is concerned about blaspheming the Holy Spirit has a proper heart and perspective and is not guilty of the unpardonable sin. People who see God as Satan are twisted enough to be unrecoverable.

Mark 3:31-35

> [31]His mother and his brothers came, and standing outside, they sent to him, calling him. [32]A multitude was sitting around him, and they

told him, "Behold, your mother, your brothers, and your sisters[16] are outside looking for you."

[33]He answered them, "Who are my mother and my brothers?" [34]Looking around at those who sat around him, he said, "Behold, my mother and my brothers! [35]For whoever does the will of God, the same is my brother, and my sister, and mother."

1. Some people teach that his mother, Mary, was a perpetual virgin. How could this be if Jesus had brothers?

Mark 6:3 mentions the names of Jesus' brothers. Those who teach that Mary was a perpetual virgin teach that his brothers were sons of Joseph from a previous marriage and that they were Jesus' step-brothers.

Mary was a virgin when Jesus was born and the conception was miraculous. This fulfilled Old Testament prophesy (Isaiah 7:14). There is no teaching in the Bible that says Mary had to remain a virgin. There are religious traditions within Christianity that see sex as impure even in marriage. To these people, sex is only for procreation. In order for them to see Mary as pure, she had to be a virgin her entire life.

Matthew 1:25 states that Joseph had no union with Mary "until" Jesus was born. This implies there was a union after Jesus was born. Mary would be no less pure because of it. Had there never been a union, Matthew would have said Joseph had no union with her.

---

[16] 3:32 TR omits "your sisters."

Chapter 4

Mark 4:1-20

[1]Again he began to teach by the seaside. A great multitude was gathered to him, so that he entered into a boat in the sea, and sat down. All the multitude were on the land by the sea. [2]He taught them many things in parables, and told them in his teaching, [3]"Listen! Behold, the farmer went out to sow, [4]and it happened, as he sowed, some seed fell by the road, and the birds[17] came and devoured it. [5]Others fell on the rocky ground, where it had little soil, and immediately it sprang up, because it had no depth of soil. [6]When the sun had risen, it was scorched; and because it had no root, it withered away. [7]Others fell among the thorns, and the thorns grew up, and choked it, and it yielded no fruit. [8]Others fell into the good ground, and yielded fruit, growing up and increasing. Some brought forth thirty times, some sixty times, and some one hundred times as much." [9]He said, "Whoever has ears to hear, let him hear."

[10]When he was alone, those who were around him with the twelve asked him about the parables. [11]He said to them, "To you is given the mystery of the kingdom of God, but to those who are outside, all things are done in parables, [12]that 'seeing they may see, and not perceive; and hearing they may hear, and not understand; lest

---

[17]   4:4: TR adds "of the air."

perhaps they should turn again, and their sins should be forgiven them.'"[18]

[13]He said to them, "Don't you understand this parable? How will you understand all of the parables? [14]The farmer sows the word. [15]The ones by the road are the ones where the word is sown; and when they have heard, immediately Satan comes, and takes away the word which has been sown in them. [16]These in the same way are those who are sown on the rocky places, who, when they have heard the word, immediately receive it with joy. [17]They have no root in themselves, but are short-lived. When oppression or persecution arises because of the word, immediately they stumble. [18]Others are those who are sown among the thorns. These are those who have heard the word, [19]and the cares of this age, and the deceitfulness of riches, and the lusts of other things entering in choke the word, and it becomes unfruitful. [20]Those which were sown on the good ground are those who hear the word, and accept it, and bear fruit, some thirty times, some sixty times, and some one hundred times."

1. In the parable, what does the seed represent?

According to verse 14, the seed is the Word of God.

2. What do the different soils represent?

The different soils represent people and how they receive the Word of God. There are four types of people or four responses to the Word of God.

The first soil represents people who do not receive the Word of God. They are hard, and it bounces off of them like a seed bouncing off a sidewalk. How do you see this today?

The second soil represents people who hear the Word of God, receive it at first, but soon fall away. How do you see this today?

---

[18]   4:12 Isaiah 6:9–10

The third soil represents people who hear the Word, receive it, but the cares of this world choke the Word. How do you see this today?

The fourth soil represents people who hear the Word, and it grows up in them and produces fruit. How do you see this today?

John 15:5-8

> [5]I am the vine. You are the branches. He who remains in me, and I in him, the same bears much fruit, for apart from me you can do nothing. [6]If a man doesn't remain in me, he is thrown out as a branch, and is withered; and they gather them, throw them into the fire, and they are burned. [7]If you remain in me, and my words remain in you, you will ask whatever you desire, and it will be done for you. [8]"In this is my Father glorified, that you bear much fruit; and so you will be my disciples.

3. Are all four soils saved? Which are and which are not?

According to John 15:5-8, only branches that bare fruit will be saved.

4. What does it mean to bear fruit?

There are two schools of thought. One says that fruit is actions that come from faith. Fruit could be helping people, like feeding the hungry, clothing the naked, caring for the sick, or encouraging those in despair.

Galatians 5:22-23

> But the fruit of the Spirit is love, joy, peace, patience, kindness, goodness, faithfulness,[19] gentleness, and self-control. Against such things there is no law.

The other school of thought says that bearing fruit is converting others to Christianity. If the Word of God is the seed, then the plant that

---

[19]   5:22 or faithfulness

grows up will bear more fruit by spreading more of the Word of God and producing new Christians.

5. Can someone who is hard like the first soil become softer like the second soil? How?

Yes, but they have to hear the Word of God and listen to it.

6. Can someone who is like the second soil become like the third and fourth soil? How?

They have to continue receiving the Word of God and not hear it only once.

7. Can someone who is like the third soil become like the fourth soil and bear fruit? How?

They need to keep their eyes focused on what is important and not be distracted by materialism and greed and the cares of this world. They must see life and the world from God's perspective and value what is truly valuable and ignore what is unimportant.

8. Can people change?

Mark 4:10-12,

> [10]When he was alone, those who were around him with the twelve asked him about the parables. [11]He said to them, "To you is given the mystery of the kingdom of God, but to those who are outside, all things are done in parables, [12]that 'seeing they may see, and not perceive; and hearing they may hear, and not understand; lest perhaps they should turn again, and their sins should be forgiven them.'"[20]

12. Why did Jesus speak in parables? It almost sounds like Jesus did not want people to understand.

---

[20]   4:12 Isaiah 6:9-10

Parables are an effective tool for separating the people who truly want to find God from those who do not care. The book of Matthew records that the disciples asked Jesus the same question.

Matthew 13:10-17

[10]The disciples came, and said to him, "Why do you speak to them in parables?"

[11]He answered them, "To you it is given to know the mysteries of the kingdom of Heaven, but it is not given to them. [12]For whoever has, to him will be given, and he will have abundance, but whoever doesn't have, from him will be taken away even that which he has. [13]Therefore I speak to them in parables, because seeing they don't see, and hearing, they don't hear, neither do they understand. [14]In them the prophecy of Isaiah is fulfilled, which says,
    'By hearing you will hear,
        and will in no way understand;
    Seeing you will see,
        and will in no way perceive:
    [15]for this people's heart has grown callous,
        their ears are dull of hearing,
    they have closed their eyes;
        or else perhaps they might perceive with their eyes,
    hear with their ears,
        understand with their heart,
    and should turn again;
        and I would heal them.'[21]
[16]"But blessed are your eyes, for they see; and your ears, for they hear. [17]For most certainly I tell you that many prophets and righteous men desired to see the things which you see, and didn't see them; and to hear the things which you hear, and didn't hear them.

The people who are truly interested listen to the parables and figure them out and learn and grow. The other people are like the first soil. The Word of God bounces off their hard hearts.

---

[21]   13:15 Isaiah 6:9-10

Mark 4:21-25

[21]He said to them, "Is the lamp brought to be put under a basket[22] or under a bed? Isn't it put on a stand? [22]For there is nothing hidden, except that it should be made known; neither was anything made secret, but that it should come to light. [23]If any man has ears to hear, let him hear."

[24]He said to them, "Take heed what you hear. With whatever measure you measure, it will be measured to you, and more will be given to you who hear. [25]For whoever has, to him will more be given, and he who doesn't have, even that which he has will be taken away from him."

1. **What do you think Jesus means with these statements about a lamp under a basket and a secret that comes to light?**

Jesus is saying the secret things are meant to be disclosed. Things said in parables are meant to be explained. If someone is capable of hearing the truth, let him or her hear it.

2. **What happens to the person who hears the secret things and understands them?**

The person who understands has a greater responsibility and is held in higher accountability. That person will also be given even greater understanding. The person who ignores God and His Word, even the small understanding he has will be taken away.

Mark 4:26-29

[26]He said, "The kingdom of God is as if a man should cast seed on the earth, [27]and should sleep and rise night and day, and the seed should spring up and grow, he doesn't know how. [28]For the earth bears fruit: first the blade, then the ear, then the full grain in the ear.

---

[22]　4:21 literally, a modion, a dry measuring basket containing about a peck (about 9 liters).

²⁹But when the fruit is ripe, immediately he puts forth the sickle, because the harvest has come."

1. How can Mark start using the phrase ""kingdom of God" without explaining it?

Mark obviously thought his readers would know what the phrase meant without explanation. The great irony in this book is that no one really understood what Jesus was talking about when he used the phrase. They thought they understood, but each group had a different concept. Their concepts were based on their paradigm. Their paradigm was their set of beliefs, which caused them to put facts together in different ways. This is a major theme in this study guide and will be completely explained in Mark 6.

2. What does the phrase "kingdom of God" mean to you?

(Note: People will share all kinds of answers. Some will say, "Everyone who follows God." Others will say, "the church.")

3. What is the harvest Jesus is talking about, and when will it happen?

When all the people who are in the kingdom are ready, the harvest will occur. (Some participants may ask about end times and pre-millennialism at this point. Those topics will be covered in Mark 13.)

Matthew records a couple of additional parables Jesus told about the kingdom of God.

Matthew 13:24-30

²⁴He set another parable before them, saying, "The kingdom of Heaven is like a man who sowed good seed in his field, ²⁵but while people slept, his enemy came and sowed darnel weeds²³ also among

---

²³   13:25 darnel is a weed grass (probably bearded darnel or lolium temulentum) that looks very much like wheat until it is mature, when the

the wheat, and went away. [26]But when the blade sprang up and brought forth fruit, then the darnel weeds appeared also. [27]The servants of the householder came and said to him, 'Sir, didn't you sow good seed in your field? Where did this darnel come from?'

[28]"He said to them, 'An enemy has done this.'

"The servants asked him, 'Do you want us to go and gather them up?'

[29]"But he said, 'No, lest perhaps while you gather up the darnel weeds, you root up the wheat with them. [30]Let both grow together until the harvest, and in the harvest time I will tell the reapers, "First, gather up the darnel weeds, and bind them in bundles to burn them; but gather the wheat into my barn."

1. Why does Matthew use the phrase "kingdom of Heaven" instead of the phrase Mark uses, "kingdom of God"? Are they talking about the same thing?

Matthew was writing for a Jewish audience. In their religion, it was sacrilegious to speak the name of God. It became Jewish tradition to substitute "heaven" for "God." In our culture, many people will say "For heaven's sake" instead of saying "For God's sake." In a similar fashion, Matthew uses the term ""kingdom of Heaven."

2. Who are the weeds, and who is the wheat today?

The two plants look alike until they bear fruit (grain). The wheat today is the people who bear fruit. The weeds are people who do not bear fruit.

3. Do you think it is better to be in the bundles or in the barn?

Being in the barn is a metaphor for going to heaven.

---

difference becomes very apparent.

Matthew 13:47–52

[47]"Again, the kingdom of Heaven is like a dragnet, that was cast into the sea, and gathered some fish of every kind, [48]which, when it was filled, they drew up on the beach. They sat down, and gathered the good into containers, but the bad they threw away. [49]So will it be in the end of the world. The angels will come forth, and separate the wicked from among the righteous, [50]and will cast them into the furnace of fire. There will be the weeping and the gnashing of teeth."

[51]Jesus said to them, "Have you understood all these things?"

They answered him, "Yes, Lord."

[52]He said to them, "Therefore every scribe who has been made a disciple in the kingdom of Heaven is like a man who is a householder, who brings out of his treasure new and old things."

1. What do these parables say about life? What is life?

Over and over, Jesus describes life as a test or separation. The wheat and the weeds have to be separated. The good fish have to be separated from the bad fish. You cannot tell which person is good or bad until they live their life. Life is all about choices. You have exactly the life you chose. Your choices show exactly what is in your heart.

Mark 4:30–32

[30]He said, "How will we liken the kingdom of God? Or with what parable will we illustrate it? [31]It's like a grain of mustard seed, which, when it is sown in the earth, though it is less than all the seeds that are on the earth, [32]yet when it is sown, grows up, and becomes greater than all the herbs, and puts out great branches, so that the birds of the sky can lodge under its shadow."

1. What does this tell you about the kingdom of God?

It starts out small and grows bigger than all other kingdoms and becomes a blessing to all inhabitants.

Mark 4:33-34

[33] With many such parables he spoke the word to them, as they were able to hear it. [34] Without a parable he didn't speak to them; but privately to his own disciples he explained everything.

1. Why did Jesus use parables and only parables?

Parables help the separation process. People who want to learn hear. People who don't ignore.

Mark 4:35-41

[35] On that day, when evening had come, he said to them, "Let's go over to the other side." [36] Leaving the multitude, they took him with them, even as he was, in the boat. Other small boats were also with him. [37] A big wind storm arose, and the waves beat into the boat, so much that the boat was already filled. [38] He himself was in the stern, asleep on the cushion, and they woke him up, and told him, "Teacher, don't you care that we are dying?"

[39] He awoke, and rebuked the wind, and said to the sea, "Peace! Be still!"

The wind ceased, and there was a great calm. [40] He said to them, "Why are you so afraid? How is it that you have no faith?"

[41] They were greatly afraid, and said to one another, "Who then is this, that even the wind and the sea obey him?"

1. In Mark 6:7, Jesus tells the Twelve to go out and preach. He gives them authority or power to do certain miraculous signs. The story from Mark 4:35 to Mark 6:7 is about Jesus performing miracles. This account of calming the storm is one of the focal points in Mark because it is not just about what Jesus can do. It is about who Jesus is. That is the point of the book of Mark.

2. **Imagine you are on this boat on a large lake in a storm at night. The waves are high enough to be coming over the side. You have some disciples in the group who are fishermen and are used to being on the lake. But even those men are afraid. Where is Jesus?**

In the back of the boat, asleep on a cushion.

3. **How could Jesus be asleep in a storm like that?**

He had faith. He knew they were not going to drown. He was, therefore, at peace.

4. **Why did the disciples wake Jesus?**

They were afraid. It is clear from their reaction after the storm is calmed that they did not expect Jesus to do what he did. But they woke him because they thought the ship was going to sink and they were going to die.

5. **Imagine one of the disciples waking Jesus and saying, "Teacher, don't you care that we are dying?" Imagine Jesus looking around a bit, rubbing his eyes, looking at the wind and waves and then at the disciples, and standing up in the back of the boat and saying, "Peace. Be still." Imagine all the massive energy of that storm dissipating in a matter of seconds and the wind falling off to calm air, and the waves settling down until the water was like glass. Then Jesus turned and looked at the disciples and said, "Why are you so afraid? Don't you have faith?"**

The very next verse says, "They were greatly afraid," or "they were terrified," and they asked each other, "Who is this? The wind and waves obey him! Who is this?" See, that is the central question in Mark. The whole book of Mark is about who Jesus is, and the twelve disciples are asking because they don't know who Jesus is. They thought they knew.

Imagine twelve men scrambling on top of each other to see who can get to the other end of the boat the fastest. He terrified them. Why were they terrified?

The Jews believed God could calm the waves of the sea.

Psalm 89:8-9

> [8]The Lord, God of Armies, who is a mighty one, like you?
>   Yah, your faithfulness is around you.
> [9]You rule the pride of the sea.
>   When its waves rise up, you calm them.

They believed only God could calm a raging sea. The disciples believed Jesus was a good teacher. They woke him saying, "Teacher, don't you care if we drown?" At this point, they may have believed he was the Messiah who was prophesied in the Old Testament to come and save Israel. They never expected Jesus to do what only God could do.

When they sit there in the raging calm, staring eye-to-eye with Jesus, they ask each other, "Who is this? Are we in a boat with a good teacher? Are we in a boat with the Messiah? Or, are we sitting in a boat with God?" You bet they were terrified.

Chapter 5

Mark 5:1-20

[1]They came to the other side of the sea, into the country of the Gadarenes. [2]When he had come out of the boat, immediately a man with an unclean spirit met him out of the tombs. [3]He lived in the tombs. Nobody could bind him any more, not even with chains, [4]because he had been often bound with fetters and chains, and the chains had been torn apart by him, and the fetters broken in pieces. Nobody had the strength to tame him. [5]Always, night and day, in the tombs and in the mountains, he was crying out, and cutting himself with stones. [6]When he saw Jesus from afar, he ran and bowed down to him, [7]and crying out with a loud voice, he said, "What have I to do with you, Jesus, you Son of the Most High God? I adjure you by God, don't torment me." [8]For he said to him, "Come out of the man, you unclean spirit!"

[9]He asked him, "What is your name?"

He said to him, "My name is Legion, for we are many." [10]He begged him much that he would not send them away out of the country. [11]Now on the mountainside there was a great herd of pigs feeding. [12]All the demons begged him, saying, "Send us into the pigs, that we may enter into them."

[13]At once Jesus gave them permission. The unclean spirits came out and entered into the pigs. The herd of about two thousand rushed down

the steep bank into the sea, and they were drowned in the sea. [14]Those who fed them fled, and told it in the city and in the country.

The people came to see what it was that had happened. [15]They came to Jesus, and saw him who had been possessed by demons sitting, clothed, and in his right mind, even him who had the legion; and they were afraid. [16]Those who saw it declared to them how it happened to him who was possessed by demons, and about the pigs. [17]They began to beg him to depart from their region.

[18]As he was entering into the boat, he who had been possessed by demons begged him that he might be with him. [19]He didn't allow him, but said to him, "Go to your house, to your friends, and tell them what great things the Lord has done for you, and how he had mercy on you."

[20]He went his way, and began to proclaim in Decapolis how Jesus had done great things for him, and everyone marveled.

1. **Can anyone guess what this is? This is the first recorded occurrence of . . . ?**

Deviled ham.

2. **What can you tell about the Gadarenes from this account? Are they Gentiles or Jews?**

They were Gentiles. The Old Testament dietary laws prohibited Jews from eating pork (Leviticus 11:7-8). Jews did not keep herds of pigs.

3. **In verses 14-17, the people pleaded with Jesus to leave their region. Why?**

Maybe they were afraid of Jesus. It says no one could handle the man with demons. It seems they were even more afraid of Jesus. How are people like the Gadarenes today?

People have many problems today that plague them. People are afraid of Jesus today. People sometimes prefer the demons that are familiar to the power of Jesus that is not so familiar.

4. **In verses 18-20, Jesus told the demon-possessed man who was healed to go home and tell his family how much God had done for him. In Mark 1:25, 1:34 and 3:11-12, Jesus would not let the evil spirits tell who he was. When Jesus healed the man with leprosy (Mark 1:44), he commanded the man not to tell anyone what had happened. Why did Jesus command this man to tell his family when he commanded so many others to remain silent?**

The answer will be revealed in chapter 6. A major difference is that this man was a Gentile and the others were Jews. But why that mattered will be revealed in chapter 6.

5. **In verse 7, what did the demon say about Jesus, and how did the demon's declaration fit into the theme of Mark, "Who is Jesus?"**

He, or they, said that Jesus was the Son of the Most High God. It is ironic that up to this point, only the demons knew who Jesus was.

Mark 5:21-43

> [21]When Jesus had crossed back over in the boat to the other side, a great multitude was gathered to him; and he was by the sea. [22]Behold, one of the rulers of the synagogue, Jairus by name, came; and seeing him, he fell at his feet, [23]and begged him much, saying, "My little daughter is at the point of death. Please come and lay your hands on her, that she may be made healthy, and live."

> [24]He went with him, and a great multitude followed him, and they pressed upon him on all sides. [25]A certain woman, who had an issue of blood for twelve years, [26]and had suffered many things by many physicians, and had spent all that she had, and was no better, but rather grew worse, [27]having heard the things concerning Jesus, came up behind him in the crowd, and touched his clothes. [28]For she said,

"If I just touch his clothes, I will be made well." [29]Immediately the flow of her blood was dried up, and she felt in her body that she was healed of her affliction.

[30]Immediately Jesus, perceiving in himself that the power had gone out from him, turned around in the crowd, and asked, "Who touched my clothes?"

[31]His disciples said to him, "You see the multitude pressing against you, and you say, 'Who touched me?'"

[32]He looked around to see her who had done this thing. [33]But the woman, fearing and trembling, knowing what had been done to her, came and fell down before him, and told him all the truth.

[34]He said to her, "Daughter, your faith has made you well. Go in peace, and be cured of your disease."

[35]While he was still speaking, people came from the synagogue ruler's house saying, "Your daughter is dead. Why bother the Teacher any more?"

[36]But Jesus, when he heard the message spoken, immediately said to the ruler of the synagogue, "Don't be afraid, only believe." [37]He allowed no one to follow him, except Peter, James, and John the brother of James. [38]He came to the synagogue ruler's house, and he saw an uproar, weeping, and great wailing. [39]When he had entered in, he said to them, "Why do you make an uproar and weep? The child is not dead, but is asleep."

[40]They ridiculed him. But he, having put them all out, took the father of the child, her mother, and those who were with him, and went in where the child was lying. [41]Taking the child by the hand, he said to her, "Talitha cumi!" which means, being interpreted, "Girl, I tell you, get up!"

[42]Immediately the girl rose up and walked, for she was twelve years old. They were amazed with great amazement. [43]He strictly

ordered them that no one should know this, and commanded that something should be given to her to eat.

1. Do you think it was hard for a synagogue ruler to go to Jesus for help?

Yes. Synagogue rulers were part of the official religion, and the leaders of the official religion were opposing Jesus more and more.

2. Jairus' little daughter was at the point of death. What was he feeling at this point in the story?

Panic, fear, desperation.

3. How do you think Jairus felt when Jesus agreed to go with him?

Hopeful.

4. How do you think Jairus felt when Jesus stopped to help the woman?

Resentful, panicked, frustrated. He thought his little girl might have a chance when Jesus agreed to go. Now, time was slipping away.

5. What does this story teach you about God's timetable?

We often do not see things the way God sees them. Our priorities are often not God's priorities.

6. Why did Jesus ignore the men who came from Jairus' house to tell him the little girl had died?

They told what they thought was the truth about the situation, but it was from their perspective without faith. When people have little faith, it is often hard to see the true situation.

7. The crowd laughed at Jesus. How is that similar to today?

People laugh at Jesus and Christians today. We are laughed at because we believe God created the universe and the world and everything in it. Jesus presented the crowd with an unbelievable statement. He said the dead girl was not dead. The crowd knew two things for certain. The little girl was dead, and no one who is dead comes back to life. It was unbelievable that she could live again. That does not happen in this reality. What is true is often different than what the crowd believes. What is true sometimes takes a measure of faith to go with it to see it.

8. If you were Jairus and saw your little girl brought back to life, how would you feel?

Ecstatic, overjoyed, awed, humbled, elated, etc.

9. How would you feel if Jesus raised you back to life?

Same type of emotions and that is the point. Jesus has the power to bring everyone back to life. That is the promise of the good news. Jesus is the answer to death.

Chapter 6

Mark 6:1-6a

¹He went out from there. He came into his own country, and his disciples followed him. ²When the Sabbath had come, he began to teach in the synagogue, and many hearing him were astonished, saying, "Where did this man get these things?" and, "What is the wisdom that is given to this man, that such mighty works come about by his hands? ³Isn't this the carpenter, the son of Mary, and brother of James, Joses, Judah, and Simon? Aren't his sisters here with us?" They were offended at him.

⁴Jesus said to them, "A prophet is not without honor, except in his own country, and among his own relatives, and in his own house." ⁵He could do no mighty work there, except that he laid his hands on a few sick people, and healed them. ⁶He marveled because of their unbelief.

1. Did Mary have other children besides Jesus?

Some churches believe and teach that Mary was a perpetual virgin. They generally take a position that abstinence from sex, or celibacy, is more pure than engaging in sex inside of marriage. Combining this preconceived idea with the desire to see Mary as ultimately pure in all aspects of life, the conclusion is drawn that she was a perpetual virgin.

Could the siblings of Jesus be Joseph's children from a previous marriage? Possibly. Could they be adopted children? Possibly. The point of the text is that the people in this town knew Jesus and his family very well, and they did not respect him because he was "one of them."

Luke 1:26-38 tells us that Mary was a virgin when Jesus was born. Matthew 1:18-25 tells us that "Joseph had no union with her until she gave birth to a son." To most, the use of, "until" implies that there was union after Jesus' birth.

At stake is the sanctity of physical intimacy in marriage and whether abstinence and perpetual virginity are more pure than intimacy in marriage. Obviously, people who have taken a vow of celibacy have a strong opinion on the matter.

2. Why do you think the people of his home town took offense at Jesus?

Note that the town's people did not say, "Isn't this one of the carpenters family?" They said, "Isn't this Mary's son?" Since they claimed to know four other brothers, it seems odd that they would single out this one son, calling him "Mary's son." Obviously, they are referring to the story that Jesus was not Joseph's offspring.

The point is that a prophet is without honor in his home town and among his own family.

Mark 6:6b-13

> He went around the villages teaching. [7]He called to himself the twelve, and began to send them out two by two; and he gave them authority over the unclean spirits. [8]He commanded them that they should take nothing for their journey, except a staff only: no bread, no wallet, no money in their purse, [9]but to wear sandals, and not put on two tunics. [10]He said to them, "Wherever you enter into a house, stay there until you depart from there. [11]Whoever will not receive you nor hear you, as you depart from there, shake off the dust that is under your feet for a testimony against them. Assuredly, I tell you, it will be more tolerable for Sodom and Gomorrah in the day of judgment than for that city!"

¹²They went out and preached that people should repent. ¹³They cast out many demons, and anointed many with oil who were sick, and healed them.

1. Why did Jesus send them out two-by-two?

It is more encouraging to do things in a team. Ecclesiastes 4:9-12.

2. Why did Jesus send them with nothing?

This was going to be a short trip, a limited commission. In Luke 22:35-38, Jesus tells the disciples to take provisions and get ready for what is about to happen because they are not going to return to Jesus. But here in Mark, they will return to Jesus in a matter of day.

3. Imagine a young person starting out in life or a young couple starting out in marriage. What would you tell them to pack in their bag to take on the journey of life?

Faith, respect, love, purity, etc.

4. What did the disciples preach as they went from town to town?

Verse 12 says they preached that people should repent.

5. Imagine two of the disciples walking into the town square and saying, "Repent, for the kingdom of God is here." Then they look at each other and say, "Well, that about covers it. Shall we go to the next town?" What did they really tell people?

They did tell people to repent, but it is likely that the message included what Jesus was doing. It is likely they were saying, "Listen to us! We have found the Messiah! The Messiah that the Old Testament prophets told us about is here. We have seen him heal the sick and cast out demons, and he even raised a little girl from the dead! You have to listen to us! We have found the Messiah who was prophesied to save Israel!"

Mark 6:14-29

[14]King Herod heard this, for his name had become known, and he said, "John the Baptizer has risen from the dead, and therefore these powers are at work in him." [15]But others said, "He is Elijah." Others said, "He is a prophet, or like one of the prophets." [16]But Herod, when he heard this, said, "This is John, whom I beheaded. He has risen from the dead." [17]For Herod himself had sent out and arrested John, and bound him in prison for the sake of Herodias, his brother Philip's wife, for he had married her. [18]For John said to Herod, "It is not lawful for you to have your brother's wife." [19]Herodias set herself against him, and desired to kill him, but she couldn't, [20]for Herod feared John, knowing that he was a righteous and holy man, and kept him safe. When he heard him, he did many things, and he heard him gladly.

[21]Then a convenient day came, that Herod on his birthday made a supper for his nobles, the high officers, and the chief men of Galilee. [22]When the daughter of Herodias herself came in and danced, she pleased Herod and those sitting with him. The king said to the young lady, "Ask me whatever you want, and I will give it to you." [23]He swore to her, "Whatever you shall ask of me, I will give you, up to half of my kingdom."

[24]She went out, and said to her mother, "What shall I ask?"

She said, "The head of John the Baptizer."

[25]She came in immediately with haste to the king, and asked, "I want you to give me right now the head of John the Baptizer on a platter."

[26]The king was exceedingly sorry, but for the sake of his oaths, and of his dinner guests, he didn't wish to refuse her. [27]Immediately the king sent out a soldier of his guard, and commanded to bring John's head, and he went and beheaded him in the prison, [28]and brought his head on a platter, and gave it to the young lady; and the young lady gave it to her mother.

²⁹When his disciples heard this, they came and took up his corpse, and laid it in a tomb.

1. **John the Baptist is an example of what sometimes happens to people who preach repentance. <u>Mark 6:16.</u> Why did Herod think Jesus was John the Baptist raised from the dead?**

Herod was consumed by guilt. He knew John was a righteous and innocent man that he murdered.

2. **What is the strangest thing guilt made you do?**

<u>Mark 6:30–31</u>

³⁰The apostles gathered themselves together to Jesus, and they told him all things, whatever they had done, and whatever they had taught. ³¹He said to them, "You come apart into a deserted place, and rest awhile." For there were many coming and going, and they had no leisure so much as to eat.

1. **In Mark 6:6b-13, Jesus sent the disciples out to preach. Here in Mark 6:30-31, the Twelve come back from their preaching mission and tell Jesus all they had done and taught. Why are there so many people around them that they cannot even eat?**

The answer is revealed in the next section.

2. **Why did Jesus take the disciples away to a deserted place?**

The answer is revealed in the next section.

3. **Why is the account of the death of John the Baptist sandwiched in between the Twelve going out to preach and them returning with huge numbers of people?**

The answer is revealed in the next section.

Mark 6:32–44

[32]They went away in the boat to a deserted place by themselves. [33]They[24] saw them going, and many recognized him and ran there on foot from all the cities. They arrived before them and came together to him. [34]Jesus came out, saw a great multitude, and he had compassion on them, because they were like sheep without a shepherd, and he began to teach them many things. [35]When it was late in the day, his disciples came to him, and said, "This place is deserted, and it is late in the day. [36]Send them away, that they may go into the surrounding country and villages, and buy themselves bread, for they have nothing to eat."

[37]But he answered them, "You give them something to eat."

They asked him, "Shall we go and buy two hundred denarii[25] worth of bread, and give them something to eat?"

[38]He said to them, "How many loaves do you have? Go see."

When they knew, they said, "Five, and two fish."

[39]He commanded them that everyone should sit down in groups on the green grass. [40]They sat down in ranks, by hundreds and by fifties. [41]He took the five loaves and the two fish, and looking up to heaven, he blessed and broke the loaves, and he gave to his disciples to set before them, and he divided the two fish among them all. [42]They all ate, and were filled. [43]They took up twelve baskets full of broken pieces and also of the fish. [44]Those who ate the loaves were[26] five thousand men.

1. **Even after Jesus took the Twelve to a deserted place, there were still 5,000 men that came to be with Jesus and the**

---

[24] 6:33 TR reads "The multitudes" instead of "They."
[25] 6:37200 denarii was about seven or eight months wages for an agricultural laborer.
[26] 6:44 TR adds "about."

Twelve. What were 5,000 men doing in a remote area sitting in groups of fifties and hundreds?

The fact that there were 5,000 men in a remote area, sitting in groups of fifty and one-hundred, suggests that the 5,000 men thought they were an army.[27] The Greek word used to describe the groups is a gardening term that means straight rows and neatly arranged sections. Mark emphasizes that there were 5,000 men and does not mention women.

Imagine you are a person living in first-century Palestine. Your country is occupied by Romans. You see Romans in the streets and hear about how they murder anyone who breaks their laws or dares to resist them. They make you carry their packs and gear like a slave. They tax your family until you don't have enough to eat. The Romans are Gentiles, and you have learned to hate them.

Next, being a good Jewish person, you go to synagogue every Saturday. You hear stories that the Messiah is going to come save Israel. On one particular Sabbath, you hear Zechariah 14:3-9 read aloud.

Zechariah 14:3, 9-17

>[3]Then the Lord will go out and fight against those nations, as when he fought in the day of battle.
>
>[9]The Lord will be King over all the earth. In that day the Lord will be one, and his name one. [10]All the land will be made like the Arabah, from Geba to Rimmon south of Jerusalem; and she will be lifted up, and will dwell in her place, from Benjamin's gate to the place of the first gate, to the corner gate, and from the tower of Hananel to the king's winepresses. [11]Men will dwell therein, and there will be no more curse; but Jerusalem will dwell safely. [12]This will be the plague with which the Lord will strike all the peoples who have warred against Jerusalem: their flesh will consume away

---

[27] Montefiore, Hugh, "Revolt in the Desert?" New Testament Studies 8 (Jan. 1962):135-41

while they stand on their feet, and their eyes will consume away in their sockets, and their tongue will consume away in their mouth. [13]It will happen in that day, that a great panic from the Lord will be among them; and they will lay hold everyone on the hand of his neighbor, and his hand will rise up against the hand of his neighbor. [14]Judah also will fight at Jerusalem; and the wealth of all the surrounding nations will be gathered together: gold, and silver, and clothing, in great abundance.

[15]So will be the plague of the horse, of the mule, of the camel, and of the donkey, and of all the animals that will be in those camps, as that plague. [16]It will happen that everyone who is left of all the nations that came against Jerusalem will go up from year to year to worship the King, the Lord of Armies, and to keep the feast of tents. [17]It will be, that whoever of all the families of the earth doesn't go up to Jerusalem to worship the King, the Lord of Armies, on them there will be no rain.

Imagine how that verse is interpreted in Roman-occupied Palestine. At another synagogue meeting, someone reads Psalm 2:1-12.

Psalm 2:1-12

[1]Why do the nations rage,
    and the peoples plot a vain thing?
[2]The kings of the earth take a stand,
    and the rulers take counsel together,
    against the Lord, and against his Anointed,[28] saying,
[3]"Let's break their bonds apart,
    and cast their cords from us."
[4]He who sits in the heavens will laugh.
    The Lord[29] will have them in derision.
[5]Then he will speak to them in his anger,
    and terrify them in his wrath:

---

[28] 2:2 The word "Anointed" is the same as the word for "Messiah" or "Christ."
[29] 2:4 The word translated "Lord" is "Adonai."

⁶"Yet I have set my King on my holy hill of Zion."
   ⁷I will tell of the decree.
The Lord said to me, "You are my son.
   Today I have become your father.
⁸Ask of me, and I will give the nations for your inheritance,
   the uttermost parts of the earth for your possession.
⁹You shall break them with a rod of iron.
   You shall dash them in pieces like a potter's vessel."
¹⁰Now therefore be wise, you kings.
   Be instructed, you judges of the earth.
¹¹Serve the Lord with fear,
   and rejoice with trembling.

Psalm 2 actually says the Son of God will rule the nations.

Psalm 72:1-20

By Solomon.
   ¹God, give the king your justice;
      your righteousness to the royal son.
   ²He will judge your people with righteousness,
      and your poor with justice.
   ³The mountains shall bring prosperity to the people.
      The hills bring the fruit of righteousness.
   ⁴He will judge the poor of the people.
      He will save the children of the needy,
      and will break the oppressor in pieces.
   ⁵They shall fear you while the sun endures;
      and as long as the moon, throughout all generations.
   ⁶He will come down like rain on the mown grass,
      as showers that water the earth.
   ⁷In his days, the righteous shall flourish,
      and abundance of peace, until the moon is no more.
   ⁸He shall have dominion also from sea to sea,
      from the River to the ends of the earth.
   ⁹Those who dwell in the wilderness shall bow before him.
      His enemies shall lick the dust.
   ¹⁰The kings of Tarshish and of the islands will bring tribute.
      The kings of Sheba and Seba shall offer gifts.

[11]Yes, all kings shall fall down before him.

All nations shall serve him.

[12]For he will deliver the needy when he cries;

the poor, who has no helper.

[13]He will have pity on the poor and needy.

He will save the souls of the needy.

[14]He will redeem their soul from oppression and violence.

Their blood will be precious in his sight.

[15]They shall live, and to him shall be given of the gold of Sheba.

Men shall pray for him continually.

They shall bless him all day long.

[16]Abundance of grain shall be throughout the land.

Its fruit sways like Lebanon.

Let it flourish, thriving like the grass of the field.

[17]His name endures forever.

His name continues as long as the sun.

Men shall be blessed by him.

All nations will call him blessed.

[18]Praise be to the Lord God, the God of Israel,

who alone does marvelous deeds.

[19]Blessed be his glorious name forever!

Let the whole earth be filled with his glory!

Amen and amen.

[20]This ends the prayers by David, the son of Jesse.

In Daniel 2, the Bible clearly predicts four world empires, with the Roman Empire being the fourth since the time of Daniel. It came to pass exactly as predicted in the book of Daniel. Daniel 2:44 predicts that God will establish his kingdom during the time of the Roman Empire.

Daniel 2:44

[44]In the days of those kings shall the God of heaven set up a kingdom which shall never be destroyed, nor shall its sovereignty be left to another people; but it shall break in pieces and consume all these kingdoms, and it shall stand forever.

Modern readers with the advantage of hindsight understand that the kingdom of God predicted here is the church and the believers following the King of Kings. The Jews who were living under brutal Roman occupation interpreted all these passages literally.

They believed that the Messiah was going to overthrow Rome. They knew that Caesar was a king over the whole known earth. They thought that the Messiah was going to defeat Rome and take Caesar's place. They knew that their ancestors defeated the armies of Egypt with God on their side. They knew that the Israelites had won military victory after victory until the Promised Land was theirs.

They knew that their land had been taken over by Babylonians, Assyrians, Medes and Persians, and Romans because the people of God had turned away from him and stopped following his laws and decrees. This is why it sounded right that John the Baptist, Jesus, and the Twelve would be preaching, "Repent, for the kingdom of God is near." In order to defeat Rome, they had to have God on their side. It was time to repent and get right with God, so they could fight in the power of God.

Mark inserted the story about the death of John the Baptist between the Twelve sent to preach and then returning with 5,000 men because it was the perfect call-to-arms. The people in Palestine knew John the Baptist was from God. Even Herod, who killed John, knew he was from God. You can hear the Jews yelling in the streets, "The puppet of the Romans killed our prophet!"

The first question we skipped was about the calling of the first disciples in chapter 1. Jesus walked up to the fishermen and said, "Come, follow me." They left the families, their boats, their jobs, everything. That is odd unless they thought they were being drafted to fight a war. The same type of thing happened in the United States during the Civil War. A sergeant would ride through the countryside and see young men working in the fields. He would say, "Come on boys, let's go fight the Yankees." They would leave everything to go to war.

Yes, the disciples thought Jesus was the Messiah, the one prophesied to come and save them. Only, they had a preconceived idea of what the Messiah was going to do. They believed the Messiah was going to physically overthrow Rome and free the Jews from Roman occupation. They did not see—they could not see—the spiritual war that was about to occur.

The disciples were not ultra-spiritual men seeking enlightenment. They were revolutionaries ready to fight against the evil Gentile Romans who were defiling their country, their women, and killing their prophet.

In Mark 3:21, Jesus' mother and family came to take charge of him because they thought he was out of his mind. If anyone should have known who Jesus was, it was Mary, his mother. She talked with the angel. She was told he was going to be the Son of the Most High God. But again, Mary would have interpreted this in the only way she knew how. She thought Jesus was going to be king over Israel. When Jesus resisted violence at every turn and continually preached about peace and loving your enemies, she and his brothers thought he was off track. They came to correct him.

On a number of occasions, Jesus would not let the demons tell who he was in front of Jewish audiences, but the Gadarene could go tell anyone and everyone. It was because the Gentile Gardarenes would not have a preconceived idea about Jesus as a military leader. But when the demons shouted, "You are the Son of the Most High God," they were creating the worst possible trouble for Jesus. The more people who bought into the preconceived idea that Jesus was supposed to be a military Messiah who would overthrow Rome, the more his message became lost and unheard.

When Jesus sent the disciples out to preach, they went into the surrounding towns and villages and told people, "Repent, for the kingdom of God is near. We have found the Messiah who was prophesied to come. He has the power of God. We saw him calm a storm on the lake. We saw him heal the sick and cast out demons. We even saw him raise the dead. We can defeat the Romans with Jesus. If you die in battle, he can raise you back to life."

Truly, with Jesus on their side, they would have been an invincible army.

When the disciples returned to Jesus, they brought an army. They brought people who were ready to fight Rome. Jesus tried to remove them from the crowds by taking them to a remote, desolate area. Still, 5,000 men followed them and sat down in groups of fifties and hundreds—battalions.

The Gospel of John gives a little more insight into the feeding of the 5,000.

John 6:10-15

> [10]Jesus said, "Have the people sit down." Now there was much grass in that place. So the men sat down, in number about five thousand. [11]Jesus took the loaves; and having given thanks, he distributed to the disciples, and the disciples to those who were sitting down; likewise also of the fish as much as they desired. [12]When they were filled, he said to his disciples, "Gather up the broken pieces which are left over, that nothing be lost." [13]So they gathered them up, and filled twelve baskets with broken pieces from the five barley loaves, which were left over by those who had eaten. [14]When therefore the people saw the sign which Jesus did, they said, "This is truly the prophet who comes into the world." [15]Jesus therefore, perceiving that they were about to come and take him by force, to make him king, withdrew again to the mountain by himself.

John plainly states that the 5,000 intended to make Jesus king by force.

2. Is the feeding of the 5,000 really about feeding the hungry?

The typical interpretation of the feeding of the 5,000 is that we should all feed the hungry. Jesus had compassion on the hungry, so we should volunteer at a soup kitchen. While feeding the hungry is central to what Jesus taught, this passage is not about compassion for hungry people. It is about taking responsibility for your actions.

Jesus knew what was about to happen. The crowd that saw themselves as an army was getting hungry. At any point, they were going to go off into the surrounding countryside and beg, borrow, or steal food from anyone and everyone. They saw it as their right. Jesus saw it as a travesty about to occur. So Jesus tells the disciples, "You give them something to eat." What he is saying is, "You brought them out here. You gathered an army. If you think this is such a good plan, you take care of them."

Mark 6:45–52

[45]Immediately he made his disciples get into the boat, and to go ahead to the other side, to Bethsaida, while he himself sent the multitude away. [46]After he had taken leave of them, he went up the mountain to pray.

[47]When evening had come, the boat was in the midst of the sea, and he was alone on the land. [48]Seeing them distressed in rowing, for the wind was contrary to them, about the fourth watch of the night he came to them, walking on the sea,[30] and he would have passed by them, [49]but they, when they saw him walking on the sea, supposed that it was a ghost, and cried out; [50]for they all saw him, and were troubled. But he immediately spoke with them, and said to them, "Cheer up! It is I![31] Don't be afraid." [51]He got into the boat with them; and the wind ceased, and they were very amazed among themselves, and marveled; [52]for they hadn't understood about the loaves, but their hearts were hardened.

[53]When they had crossed over, they came to land at Gennesaret, and moored to the shore. [54]When they had come out of the boat, immediately the people recognized him, [55]and ran around that whole region, and began to bring those who were sick, on their mats, to where they heard he was. [56]Wherever he entered, into villages, or into cities, or into the country, they laid the sick in the marketplaces, and begged him that they might touch just the fringe[32] of his garment; and as many as touched him were made well.

---

[30]   6:48 see Job 9:8
[31]   6:50 or, "I AM!"
[32]   6:56 or, tassel

1. **Jesus immediately forced the disciples to get into a boat and go. Why send the disciples away?**

Jesus is trying to prevent a massacre. They were the ones who had gathered the army. They were the spark plugs. The last time Jesus tried to get the disciples away from the crowd, everyone just followed them. This time, Jesus is staying to hold the crowd while the disciples go away.

2. **After Jesus sent everyone home, he went up into the hills to pray. Do you think he needed to pray? What do you think he talked to God about?**

He probably prayed for enlightenment—that the eyes of the disciples could be opened and they could see what he was telling them plainly. They only saw war.

3. **In verse 52, it says their hearts were hardened. Why?**

The disciples had just recruited an army. They worked hard. The Jewish people were ready to go to war because the Romans and their puppets had killed their prophet from God, John the Baptist. Now, Jesus had stopped the war. Based on their preconceived ideas, this was not right

Chapter 7

[1]Then the Pharisees, and some of the scribes gathered together to him, having come from Jerusalem. [2]Now when they saw some of his disciples eating bread with defiled, that is, unwashed, hands, they found fault. [3](For the Pharisees, and all the Jews, don't eat unless they wash their hands and forearms, holding to the tradition of the elders. [4]They don't eat when they come from the marketplace, unless they bathe themselves, and there are many other things, which they have received to hold to: washings of cups, pitchers, bronze vessels, and couches.) [5]The Pharisees and the scribes asked him, "Why don't your disciples walk according to the tradition of the elders, but eat their bread with unwashed hands?"

[6]He answered them, "Well did Isaiah prophesy of you hypocrites, as it is written,

> 'This people honors me with their lips,
>> but their heart is far from me.
> [7]But in vain do they worship me,
>> teaching as doctrines the commandments of men.'[33]

---

[33]   7:7 Isaiah 29:13

[8]"For you set aside the commandment of God, and hold tightly to the tradition of men—the washing of pitchers and cups, and you do many other such things."

(Note: This section contrasts Jesus' teaching with the religion of his day. The Pharisees were concerned with rules and rituals that were created by men, not God. They judged the disciples and tried to make them conform.)

1. What is the difference between a command of God and a tradition of man?

A command of God is written in the Bible as an imperative that should be obeyed. A tradition of men is an interpretation of how to live out the commands of God. Commands of God are binding while traditions of men are not.

2. What are some examples of man-made religious traditions that are taught as commands of God?

There is no shortage of possible answers. Guard against criticizing various denominations and their traditions.

3. In verse 7, what does it mean when it says, "But in vain do they worship me . . ."?

Their worship does no good. They will not be saved by keeping the traditions of men.

Mark 7:9-13

[9]He said to them, "Full well do you reject the commandment of God, that you may keep your tradition. [10]For Moses said, 'Honor your father and your mother;'[34] and, 'He who speaks evil of father or mother, let him be put to death.'[35] [11]But you say, 'If a man tells his father or his mother, "Whatever profit you might have received

---

[34] 7:10 Exodus 20:12; Deuteronomy 5:16
[35] 7:10 Exodus 21:17; Leviticus 20:9

from me is Corban[36], that is to say, given to God";' [12]then you no longer allow him to do anything for his father or his mother, [13]making void the word of God by your tradition, which you have handed down. You do many things like this."

1. **In this example, what was the command of God, and what was the tradition of men?**

The command of God was the fifth of the Ten Commandments, "Honor your father and mother" (Exodus 20:12). Jewish tradition said that giving money to the temple was a great act of spirituality, even if it meant your elderly parents had to go without.

2. **Jesus was teaching that the traditions of the Pharisees made void or nullified the word of God. Can that happen today? Can you think of any examples?**

There are many examples.

3. **Are all man-made rules and traditions evil?**

Some traditions, like celebrating Christmas with a decorated tree and gift-giving, are enriching. Other traditions are used to judge people and make them feel unworthy. Some traditions rob people of life. Jesus came to give us abundant life. The commands of God were intended to make our lives better by protecting us from dangerous and destructive behaviors.

Mark 7:14-23

[14]He called all the multitude to himself, and said to them, "Hear me, all of you, and understand. [15]There is nothing from outside of the man, that going into him can defile him; but the things which proceed out of the man are those that defile the man. [16]If anyone has ears to hear, let him hear!"

---

[36] 7:11 Corban is a Hebrew word for an offering devoted to God.

[17]When he had entered into a house away from the multitude, his disciples asked him about the parable. [18]He said to them, "Are you thus without understanding also? Don't you perceive that whatever goes into the man from outside can't defile him, [19]because it doesn't go into his heart, but into his stomach, then into the latrine, thus purifying all foods[37]?" [20]He said, "That which proceeds out of the man, that defiles the man. [21]For from within, out of the hearts of men, proceed evil thoughts, adulteries, sexual sins, murders, thefts, [22]covetings, wickedness, deceit, lustful desires, an evil eye, blasphemy, pride, and foolishness. [23]All these evil things come from within, and defile the man."

1. **The Jewish dietary laws from the Old Testament prevented Jews from eating pork and other foods. In this statement, Jesus freed Christians from observing the Jewish dietary laws.**

2. **What does Jesus mean when he says a person can be defiled (or, as some translations say, "unclean")?**

The Old Testament described many activities as making a person unclean. Some activities would make a person unclean until evening and others until they were ceremonial cleansed. Coming in contact with mildew or a dead body would make a person unclean. Uncleanliness meant the unclean person could not participate in temple worship. In some cases, an unclean person was required to live outside the camp until the situation changed. See Leviticus 15 for examples.

Mark 7:24-30

[24]From there he arose, and went away into the borders of Tyre and Sidon. He entered into a house, and didn't want anyone to know it, but he couldn't escape notice. [25]For a woman, whose little daughter had an unclean spirit, having heard of him, came and fell down at his feet. [26]Now the woman was a Greek, a Syrophoenician by race. She begged him that he would cast the demon out of her daughter.

---

[37] 7:19 or, making all foods clean

[27]But Jesus said to her, "Let the children be filled first, for it is not appropriate to take the children's bread and throw it to the dogs."

[28]But she answered him, "Yes, Lord. Yet even the dogs under the table eat the children's crumbs."

[29]He said to her, "For this saying, go your way. The demon has gone out of your daughter."

[30]She went away to her house, and found the child having been laid on the bed, with the demon gone out.

1. **Why do you think Jesus went into a predominantly Gentile region?**

At this point, large crowds were trying to make Jesus king by force (John 6:15). The Gentiles were not looking for a Messiah to save Israel. By focusing on Gentiles, he could escape some of the attention and let things cool down among the Jews.

2. **In Mark 7:27, Jesus uses a metaphor with children, bread, and dogs. What does each thing represent?**

The children are the Jews. The bread represents the blessing of Jesus to the Jews, and the dogs represent the Gentiles.

3. **Did Jesus call this woman, and all Gentiles, dogs?**

Jesus created a teaching moment. The Jews referred to Gentiles as dogs. Jesus was using that as beginning point to show she could be accepted and receive the blessings of the Jews by faith. This is a critical concept in the New Testament. Without this teaching, Christianity would have been a sect within Judaism and everyone who became a Christian would first have to become a Jew.

Romans 2:28-29

[28]For he is not a Jew who is one outwardly, neither is that circumcision which is outward in the flesh; [29]but he is a Jew who is one inwardly,

and circumcision is that of the heart, in the spirit not in the letter; whose praise is not from men, but from God.

Galatians 3:6-9

[6]Even as Abraham "believed God, and it was counted to him for righteousness." [7]Know therefore that those who are of faith, the same are children of Abraham. [8]The scripture, foreseeing that God would justify the Gentiles by faith, preached the Good News beforehand to Abraham, saying, "In you all the nations will be blessed."[38] [9]So then, those who are of faith are blessed with the faithful Abraham.

The woman called Jesus "Lord." This is the only time in the book of Mark that anyone calls Jesus "Lord," and a Gentile is the one doing it. (Mark, as an author, refers to Jesus as Lord in 16:19 when he is taken up into Heaven, but no one in the book calls Jesus Lord except this Gentile woman.)

The point is that a Gentile who believes Jesus is the Lord can be saved or blessed just like Abraham was blessed by God when he believed in Genesis 15:6.

Mark 7:31-37

[31]Again he departed from the borders of Tyre and Sidon, and came to the sea of Galilee, through the midst of the region of Decapolis. [32]They brought to him one who was deaf and had an impediment in his speech. They begged him to lay his hand on him. [33]He took him aside from the multitude, privately, and put his fingers into his ears, and he spat, and touched his tongue. [34]Looking up to heaven, he sighed, and said to him, "Ephphatha!" that is, "Be opened!" [35]Immediately his ears were opened, and the impediment of his tongue was released, and he spoke clearly. [36]He commanded them that they should tell no one, but the more he commanded them, so much the more widely they proclaimed

---

[38]   3:8 Genesis 12:3; 18:18; 22:18

it. ³⁷They were astonished beyond measure, saying, "He has done all things well. He makes even the deaf hear, and the mute speak!"

1. Why is Jesus being secretive and healing in private?

He was trying to avoid a war with Rome. He needed the Jewish people to know that the Messiah had come but, their preconceived ideas about him were wrong. Their preconceived ideas blind them from understanding the truth.

2. Why is it ironic that Jesus heals a man who cannot hear?

He taught his followers the truth about the Messiah, faith, and spirituality, but they did not "hear" him because of their preconceived ideas. We have preconceived ideas today that keep us from hearing the truth.

Chapter 8

Mark 8:1-10

[1]In those days, when there was a very great multitude, and they had nothing to eat, Jesus called his disciples to himself, and said to them, [2]"I have compassion on the multitude, because they have stayed with me now three days, and have nothing to eat. [3]If I send them away fasting to their home, they will faint on the way, for some of them have come a long way."

[4]His disciples answered him, "From where could one satisfy these people with bread here in a deserted place?"

[5]He asked them, "How many loaves do you have?"

They said, "Seven."

[6]He commanded the multitude to sit down on the ground, and he took the seven loaves. Having given thanks, he broke them, and gave them to his disciples to serve, and they served the multitude. [7]They had a few small fish. Having blessed them, he said to serve these also. [8]They ate, and were filled. They took up seven baskets of broken pieces that were left over. [9]Those who had eaten were about four thousand. Then he sent them away.

[10]Immediately he entered into the boat with his disciples, and came into the region of Dalmanutha.

1. Why were 4,000 people, some of whom came a long distance, with Jesus in a remote place?

They wanted to fight the Romans with the Messiah. They wanted to start a revolution to free their land and return the kingdom to Israel.

Mark 8:11-13

¹¹The Pharisees came out and began to question him, seeking from him a sign from heaven, and testing him. ¹²He sighed deeply in his spirit, and said, "Why does this generation[39] seek a sign? Most certainly I tell you, no sign will be given to this generation."

¹³He left them, and again entering into the boat, departed to the other side.

Matthew 12:38-41

³⁸Then certain of the scribes and Pharisees answered, "Teacher, we want to see a sign from you."

³⁹But he answered them, "An evil and adulterous generation seeks after a sign, but no sign will be given it but the sign of Jonah the prophet. ⁴⁰For as Jonah was three days and three nights in the belly of the whale, so will the Son of Man be three days and three nights in the heart of the earth. ⁴¹The men of Nineveh will stand up in the judgment with this generation, and will condemn it, for they repented at the preaching of Jonah; and behold, someone greater than Jonah is here.

Matthew 16:1-4

The Pharisees and Sadducees came, and testing him, asked him to show them a sign from heaven. ²But he answered them, "When it is evening, you say, 'It will be fair weather, for the sky is red.' ³In

---

[39] 8:12 The word translated "generation" here (genea) could also be translated "people," "race," or "family."

the morning, 'It will be foul weather today, for the sky is red and threatening.' Hypocrites! You know how to discern the appearance of the sky, but you can't discern the signs of the times! [4]An evil and adulterous generation seeks after a sign, and there will be no sign given to it, except the sign of the prophet Jonah."

1. Why were the Pharisees and Sadducees asking for a sign? Would they have believed in him if he performed a miracle?

The Pharisees and Sadducees, the religious leaders of the day, were asking for a sign because they wanted to discredit Jesus. They wanted to show the people that Jesus could not perform a miracle. The people loved Jesus and wanted to follow Jesus instead of them. Their power was being threatened. That made them jealous, but it was also politically dangerous. If Rome decided that Jesus was a threat to their control of Palestine, Rome would punish the Jews with a massacre. This actually happened in 70 A.D. The religious leaders were walking a fine-line between satisfying the people and satisfying Rome. Discrediting Jesus would have helped calm tensions between the Jews and Rome.

2. What was the sign of Jonah that Jesus referred to?

Jonah was in the belly of a great fish for three days (Jonah 1:17). This foreshadowed Jesus' burial in a tomb for three days. The greatest proof that Jesus is the Son of God is that Jesus was resurrected from the dead three days after being placed in a tomb. If Jesus was not raised from the dead, then Christians have believed a lie and there is no hope. If Jesus conquered death and was raised to life, then he is the Son of God and what he claimed and taught was true. All of Christianity stands or falls on the resurrection. If people, either then or now, do not believe the sign of Jonah, they have no hope.

3. What did Jesus mean when he said the men of Nineveh and the Queen of the South would rise up and condemn them?

When Jonah preached to the Ninevites, they repented. Jesus preached to the generation of the Pharisees, and they hated him. All it took for the Ninevites to repent was the preaching of Jonah. But when someone far greater than Jonah was sent to the Pharisees, they refused to believe. On Judgment Day, the Ninevites will appear much more righteous than the Pharisees. Similarly, the Queen of the South traveled great distances to hear King Solomon (1 Kings 10:1-13). On Judgment Day, she will appear much more righteous and eager to see God than the Pharisees, who had the Son of God in their midst but refused to hear him.

Mark 8:14-21

¹⁴They forgot to take bread; and they didn't have more than one loaf in the boat with them. ¹⁵He warned them, saying, "Take heed: beware of the yeast of the Pharisees and the yeast of Herod."

¹⁶They reasoned with one another, saying, "It's because we have no bread."

¹⁷Jesus, perceiving it, said to them, "Why do you reason that it's because you have no bread? Don't you perceive yet, neither understand? Is your heart still hardened? ¹⁸Having eyes, don't you see? Having ears, don't you hear? Don't you remember? ¹⁹When I broke the five loaves among the five thousand, how many baskets full of broken pieces did you take up?"

They told him, "Twelve."

²⁰"When the seven loaves fed the four thousand, how many baskets full of broken pieces did you take up?"

They told him, "Seven."

²¹He asked them, "Don't you understand, yet?"

1. **Jesus warned the disciples about the yeast of the Pharisees and the yeast of Herod. They thought he was talking about physical bread. What was he really talking about?**

In Matthew 16:5-12 and 1 Corinthians 5:6-8, the scripture says that teachings are like yeast that grows and spreads through a whole loaf.

Jesus was warning the disciples to beware of the teaching of the Pharisees and Herod.

2. Did the disciples understand what Jesus was doing and teaching?

No. He asks them if they have eyes but do not see. He asks them if they remember. He multiplied the fish and loaves to feed an army, so their assumption about having no bread could not possibly be true. He asked them if their hearts were still hard. He asked them if they still did not understand. The people closest to him did not understand because they had preconceived ideas about who he should be.

It was as if they could only see a faint glimmer and everything else was blurry.

Mark 8:22-26

> [22]He came to Bethsaida. They brought a blind man to him, and begged him to touch him. [23]He took hold of the blind man by the hand, and brought him out of the village. When he had spit on his eyes, and laid his hands on him, he asked him if he saw anything.

> [24]He looked up, and said, "I see men; for I see them like trees walking."

> [25]Then again he laid his hands on his eyes. He looked intently, and was restored, and saw everyone clearly. [26]He sent him away to his house, saying, "Don't enter into the village, nor tell anyone in the village."

1. Did it really take two tries to heal this man? Was healing this blind man so difficult for Jesus that it took two tries, or was Jesus making a point? If so, what was his point?

Mark 10:46-52

> [46]They came to Jericho. As he went out from Jericho, with his disciples and a great multitude, the son of Timaeus, Bartimaeus, a

blind beggar, was sitting by the road. [47]When he heard that it was Jesus the Nazarene, he began to cry out, and say, "Jesus, you son of David, have mercy on me!" [48]Many rebuked him, that he should be quiet, but he cried out much more, "You son of David, have mercy on me!"

[49]Jesus stood still, and said, "Call him."

They called the blind man, saying to him, "Cheer up! Get up. He is calling you!"

[50]He, casting away his cloak, sprang up, and came to Jesus.

[51]Jesus asked him, "What do you want me to do for you?"

The blind man said to him, "Rabboni,[40] that I may see again."

[52]Jesus said to him, "Go your way. Your faith has made you well."

Immediately he received his sight, and followed Jesus in the way.

In Mark 10, Jesus healed a blind man in one try. These two healings are like bookends. The sections between the first blind man and the second blind man are sections that define what it means to be the Messiah and what it means to be a follower of the Messiah.

In Mark 8:21, Jesus asks the disciples, "Do you still not understand?" Imagine Jesus taking this blind man and the disciples away from the crowd. Jesus partially heals the blind man and says, "Can you see?" The blind man says, "I only see a little bit. Everything is blurry. People look like trees walking around." Imagine Jesus turning and giving the disciples a look that said, "You are just like this blind man right now. You have eyes but only see a little." Then Jesus completely heals the blind man.

---

[40]   10:51 Rabboni is a transliteration of the Hebrew word for "great teacher."

In the very next section, Jesus is going to ask the disciples who they think he is. It is because they think he is a military leader destined to lead a revolution against Rome, and they cannot see who he really is.

There are three main sections of material between the healing of the two blind men. Jesus will make three death predictions and after each prediction, he will explain what it means to be a Christian or a follower of Jesus.

Mark 8:27–9:1

²⁷Jesus went out, with his disciples, into the villages of Caesarea Philippi. On the way he asked his disciples, "Who do men say that I am?"

²⁸They told him, "John the Baptizer, and others say Elijah, but others: one of the prophets."

²⁹He said to them, "But who do you say that I am?"

Peter answered, "You are the Christ."

³⁰He commanded them that they should tell no one about him. ³¹He began to teach them that the Son of Man must suffer many things, and be rejected by the elders, the chief priests, and the scribes, and be killed, and after three days rise again. ³²He spoke to them openly. Peter took him, and began to rebuke him. ³³But he, turning around, and seeing his disciples, rebuked Peter, and said, "Get behind me, Satan! For you have in mind not the things of God, but the things of men."

³⁴He called the multitude to himself with his disciples, and said to them, "Whoever wants to come after me, let him deny himself, and take up his cross, and follow me. ³⁵For whoever wants to save his life will lose it; and whoever will lose his life for my sake and the sake of the Good News will save it. ³⁶For what does it profit a man, to gain the whole world, and forfeit his life? ³⁷For what will a man give in exchange for his life? ³⁸For whoever will be ashamed of me and of my words in this adulterous and sinful generation, the Son of Man also will be ashamed of him, when he comes in the glory of his Father with the holy angels."

[1]He said to them, "Most certainly I tell you, there are some standing here who will in no way taste death until they see the kingdom of God come with power."

1. Why did Jesus ask his disciples, "Who do men say that I am?"

Jesus knew that the disciples did not understand who he was. Again, the fundamental theme in the book of Mark is the identity of Jesus. Jesus was trying to make the point that people had all kinds of concepts about who he was.

2. Who do people say Jesus is today?

Some say Jesus was a good teacher. Some say he was a legend and never really existed. Some say he was a confused idiot that a few people mistakenly followed.

C. S. Lewis, who was a professor at Cambridge University and once an agnostic, wrote:

> "I am trying here to prevent anyone saying the really foolish thing that people often say about Him: I'm ready to accept Jesus as a great moral teacher, but I don't accept his claim to be God. That is the one thing we must not say. A man who was merely a man and said the sort of things Jesus said would not be a great moral teacher. He would either be a lunatic—on the level with the man who says he is a poached egg—or else he would be the Devil of Hell. You must make your choice. Either this man was, and is, the Son of God, or else a madman or something worse. You can shut him up for a fool, you can spit at him and kill him as a demon or you can fall at his feet and call him Lord and God, but let us not come with any patronizing nonsense about his being a great human teacher. He has not left that open to us. He did not intend to."[41]

3. Who do you say Jesus is?

---

[41] C.S. Lewis, *Mere Christianity* (New York: The MacMillan Company, 1952), 41-42.

4. Jesus focused on the disciples understanding by asking, "Who do you say I am?" What did Peter say?

Peter proclaimed that Jesus was the Christ, which is the Greek word for Messiah. Peter was saying that Jesus is the Messiah, the one prophesied to come and save Israel. This illustrates how someone can say the truth but understand a lie.

5. Why did Jesus command them not to tell who he was?

Because they didn't understand who he was. To them, the Messiah was a military leader, an earthly king like Caesar. Their misunderstanding almost started a war with Rome.

6. After commanding them not to tell anyone he was the Messiah, what did Jesus tell them?

He taught them what it really meant to be the Messiah. The Messiah dies. Verse 32 says he spoke openly about these things. He did not speak in parables. Other translations say he spoke plainly about his death and resurrection. Jesus explained what it meant to be the Messiah. It did not mean taking Caesar's place as king of the known world. It meant being betrayed by your own people, rejected, and killed. That is what it meant to be Messiah.

7. What was Peter's reaction to this teaching?

He took Jesus aside to rebuke him. That is strong language. It means Peter and Jesus had a major confrontation. Imagine Peter taking Jesus aside and saying, "Wait a minute. You have it all wrong. The Messiah does not die. He is prophesied to become a king and save Israel. We are trying to make you king. We gathered 5,000 men in one place and 4,000 in another, and we tried to make you king by force. We are not going to let you die. We are going to give you all the kingdoms of the world, and you are going to be king!"

8. When was the last time in scripture that Jesus was offered all the kingdoms of the world?

Matthew 4:8-10

[8]Again, the devil took him to an exceedingly high mountain, and showed him all the kingdoms of the world, and their glory. [9]He said to him, "I will give you all of these things, if you will fall down and worship me."

[10]Then Jesus said to him, "Get behind me,[42] Satan! For it is written, 'You shall worship the Lord your God, and you shall serve him only.'"[43]

This is why Jesus says to Peter, "Get behind me, Satan! For you do not have the concept of God but the concept of men."

The true concept of the Messiah was that Jesus would be king over a spiritual kingdom.

9. What do you think Jesus meant in Mark 9:1 when he talked about the kingdom of God coming?

Some of them would live to see the beginning of the kingdom of God, which happened in Acts 2 on the day of Pentecost after the resurrection.

10. After he tells the disciples what it really means to be the Messiah, he tells them what it really means to be his follower. What does it take to be a Christian, a follower of Jesus?

You have to deny yourself, take up your cross, and follow Jesus' teachings.

(Note: The disciples or followers of Jesus were first called Christians in Acts 11:26. Disciples of Jesus and Christians are the same people. At times in the Gospels, the word "disciples" refers to the Twelve who were following

---

42   4:10 TR and NU read "Go away" instead of "Get behind me."
43   4:10 Deuteronomy 6:13

Jesus. In generic use of the term, disciples and Christians are two terms for the same people.)

11. What does denying yourself, taking up your cross, and following Jesus look like today?

Galatians 5:19-24

> [19]Now the works of the flesh are obvious, which are: adultery, sexual immorality, uncleanness, lustfulness, [20]idolatry, sorcery, hatred, strife, jealousies, outbursts of anger, rivalries, divisions, heresies, [21]envyings, murders, drunkenness, orgies, and things like these; of which I forewarn you, even as I also forewarned you, that those who practice such things will not inherit the kingdom of God.
>
> [22]But the fruit of the Spirit is love, joy, peace, patience, kindness, goodness, faith,[44] [23]gentleness, and self-control. Against such things there is no law. [24]Those who belong to Christ have crucified the flesh with its passions and lusts. [25]If we live by the Spirit, let's also walk by the Spirit. [26]Let's not become conceited, provoking one another, and envying one another.

There are many "sin lists" in the New Testament that illustrate the same point. Sin is all about gratifying self. Uncontrolled selfishness ruins lives. It ruins marriages and other relationships. Jesus is saying that the sinful self must be crucified on a cross. The true follower of Jesus must put to death the sinful self.

The apostle Paul, in Galatians 5:22-25, contrasts a life lived for self with a life lived in accordance with the Spirit of God. If we give ourselves to love, joy, peace, patience, etc., we will, by nature, do the things required by the Old Testament law and live lives pleasing to God—and ourselves. He said it again in 2 Corinthians 5:14-15.

---

[44] 5:22 or, faithfulness

2 Corinthians 5:14-15

[14]For the love of Christ constrains us; because we judge thus, that one died for all, therefore all died. [15]He died for all, that those who live should no longer live to themselves, but to him who for their sakes died and rose again.

If you believe that Jesus is the Son of God and that he died on a cross to forgive your sins and was raised from the dead so you could be raised from the dead and live forever also, this should compel you to no longer live for yourself but for Jesus.

Jesus said the Law is summed up in love, "Love God with all your heart, soul, mind and strength and love your neighbor as yourself," Matthew 22:34-40. If you love God and love people, you will naturally do all the things required by the Law. This is why scripture says the New Covenant is written on our hearts and based on a new Spirit that God would give us.

Christians are not commanded to follow the commandments written on stone. We are compelled by gratitude to follow the Spirit and walk in love. Crucifying selfishness and living in love is what it looks like to follow Jesus today.

Chapter 9

²After six days Jesus took with him Peter, James, and John, and brought them up onto a high mountain privately by themselves, and he was changed into another form in front of them. ³His clothing became glistening, exceedingly white, like snow, such as no launderer on earth can whiten them. ⁴Elijah and Moses appeared to them, and they were talking with Jesus.

⁵Peter answered Jesus, "Rabbi, it is good for us to be here. Let's make three tents: one for you, one for Moses, and one for Elijah." ⁶For he didn't know what to say, for they were very afraid.

⁷A cloud came, overshadowing them, and a voice came out of the cloud, "This is my beloved Son. Listen to him."

⁸Suddenly looking around, they saw no one with them any more, except Jesus only.

⁹As they were coming down from the mountain, he commanded them that they should tell no one what things they had seen, until after the Son of Man had risen from the dead. ¹⁰They kept this saying to themselves, questioning what the "rising from the dead" meant.

¹¹They asked him, saying, "Why do the scribes say that Elijah must come first?"

[12]He said to them, "Elijah indeed comes first, and restores all things. How is it written about the Son of Man, that he should suffer many things and be despised? [13]But I tell you that Elijah has come, and they have also done to him whatever they wanted to, even as it is written about him."

1. Why did Jesus take Peter, James, and John up on a mountain? Why these three and not all twelve?

It may have been that these three were ready to see and hear what was about to happen. It may have been that these three were being singled out as leaders. It may have been that these three were more stubbornly committed to their preconceived ideas and needed more convincing than the others.

2. Why did Moses and Elijah appear to these three instead of Abraham or King David?

In Jewish thought, the Law and the Prophets governed their lives and shaped their perspectives.

Romans 3:21

[21]But now apart from the law, a righteousness of God has been revealed, being testified by the law and the prophets;

Acts 3:22-26

[22]For Moses indeed said to the fathers, 'the Lord God will raise up a prophet for you from among your brothers, like me. You shall listen to him in all things whatever he says to you. [23]It will be, that every soul that will not listen to that prophet will be utterly destroyed from among the people.'[45] [24]Yes, and all the prophets from Samuel and those who followed after, as many as have spoken, they also told of these days. [25]You are the children of the prophets, and of the covenant which God made with our fathers, saying to Abraham,

---

[45]   3:23 Deuteronomy 18:15,18-19

'In your seed will all the families of the earth be blessed.'[46] [26]God, having raised up his servant, Jesus, sent him to you first, to bless you, in turning away everyone of you from your wickedness."

Luke 24:25-27

[25]He said to them, "Foolish men, and slow of heart to believe in all that the prophets have spoken! [26]Didn't the Christ have to suffer these things and to enter into his glory?" [27]Beginning from Moses and from all the prophets, he explained to them in all the Scriptures the things concerning himself.

Moses and Elijah represented, or personified, the Law and the Prophets. The Jews, including Peter, James, and John, listened to and followed the Law and Prophets.

3. Why was Peter's comment considered out of place or inappropriate?

Peter was not offering to put up three shelters; he was offering to build three tabernacles or shrines. He wanted to honor the three of them. In his mind, he was trying to elevate Jesus to level of Moses and Elijah. What Peter did not realize was how far above Moses and Elijah Jesus was.

4. Who spoke from the cloud?

God. Since the time of the wilderness wanderings in the Exodus and in the temple, God's presence has been associated with the cloud that went before the Israelites to guide them. The cloud symbolized God's presence.

5. Why did God tell Peter, James, and John to listen to Jesus, especially in the presence of Moses and Elijah?

Peter, James, John, and all good Jews were devoted to listening to the Law and the Prophets. God commanded a change. Now, they were commanded to listen to the Son of God.

---

[46]   3:25 Genesis 22:18; 26:4

6. What was the symbolic meaning of Moses and Elijah disappearing, leaving the three alone with Jesus?

By showing them Moses and Elijah, God showed Peter, James, and John the essence of their religious authority and commanded them to listen to Jesus instead. Then, Moses and Elijah disappeared, and they were left with Jesus. This symbolized that their religious authority should now be Jesus, the Son of God.

7. This time, when Jesus commanded them not to tell anyone, what did they do?

For the first time, they kept quiet. Perhaps the Transfiguration produced the intended change in them.

8. In verse 11, why did they ask about Elijah coming first, before the coming of the Messiah, which was taught in Jewish culture?

Malachi 4:5-6

[5]Behold, I will send you Elijah the prophet before the great and terrible day of the Lord comes. [6]He will turn the hearts of the fathers to the children, and the hearts of the children to their fathers, lest I come and strike the earth with a curse."

The scribes, or teachers of the law, in the synagogues were quoting this verse in Malachi and telling people that Elijah was going to return to prepare the way for the Messiah. Peter, James, and John were asking Jesus if the Transfiguration was the fulfillment of the Elijah prophecy. Jesus told them that John the Baptist was the fulfillment of the Elijah prophecy.

Matthew 11:11-14

[11]Most certainly I tell you, among those who are born of women there has not arisen anyone greater than John the Baptizer; yet he who is least in the kingdom of Heaven is greater than he. [12]From the days of John the Baptizer until now, the kingdom of Heaven suffers

violence, and the violent take it by force.[47] [13]For all the prophets and the law prophesied until John. [14]If you are willing to receive it, this is Elijah, who is to come.

Mark 9:14-29

[14]Coming to the disciples, he saw a great multitude around them, and scribes questioning them. [15]Immediately all the multitude, when they saw him, were greatly amazed, and running to him greeted him. [16]He asked the scribes, "What are you asking them?"

[17]One of the multitude answered, "Teacher, I brought to you my son, who has a mute spirit; [18]and wherever it seizes him, it throws him down, and he foams at the mouth, and grinds his teeth, and wastes away. I asked your disciples to cast it out, and they weren't able."

[19]He answered him, "Unbelieving generation, how long shall I be with you? How long shall I bear with you? Bring him to me."

[20]They brought him to him, and when he saw him, immediately the spirit convulsed him, and he fell on the ground, wallowing and foaming at the mouth.

[21]He asked his father, "How long has it been since this has come to him?"

He said, "From childhood. [22]Often it has cast him both into the fire and into the water, to destroy him. But if you can do anything, have compassion on us, and help us."

[23]Jesus said to him, "If you can believe, all things are possible to him who believes."

[24]Immediately the father of the child cried out with tears, "I believe. Help my unbelief!"

---

[47]   11:12 or, plunder it.

²⁵When Jesus saw that a multitude came running together, he rebuked the unclean spirit, saying to him, "You mute and deaf spirit, I command you, come out of him, and never enter him again!"

²⁶Having cried out, and convulsed greatly, it came out of him. The boy became like one dead; so much that most of them said, "He is dead." ²⁷But Jesus took him by the hand, and raised him up; and he arose.

²⁸When he had come into the house, his disciples asked him privately, "Why couldn't we cast it out?" ²⁹He said to them, "This kind can come out by nothing, except by prayer and fasting."

1. Do you think there are evil spirits like this today?

The Bible tells us we are fighting against forces of evil.

Ephesians 6:10–12

¹⁰Finally, be strong in the Lord, and in the strength of his might. ¹¹Put on the whole armor of God, that you may be able to stand against the wiles of the devil. ¹²For our wrestling is not against flesh and blood, but against the principalities, against the powers, against the world's rulers of the darkness of this age, and against the spiritual forces of wickedness in the heavenly places.

The majority of people in the world today believe in evil spirits, and they go to great lengths to protect themselves from them.

Some people who only believe in science, facts, and empirical evidence, claim that in primitive cultures, any terrifying medical condition was considered the work of evil spirits.

Matthew 17:14–21

¹⁴When they came to the multitude, a man came to him, kneeling down to him, saying, ¹⁵"Lord, have mercy on my son, for he is epileptic, and suffers grievously; for he often falls into the fire, and

often into the water. [16]So I brought him to your disciples, and they could not cure him."

[17]Jesus answered, "Faithless and perverse generation! How long will I be with you? How long will I bear with you? Bring him here to me." [18]Jesus rebuked him, the demon went out of him, and the boy was cured from that hour.

[19]Then the disciples came to Jesus privately, and said, "Why weren't we able to cast it out?"

[20]He said to them, "Because of your unbelief. For most certainly I tell you, if you have faith as a grain of mustard seed, you will tell this mountain, 'Move from here to there,' and it will move; and nothing will be impossible for you. [21]But this kind doesn't go out except by prayer and fasting."

In verse 15, the father said the boy was an epileptic. He was saying his son had epilepsy. The father brought his son to the disciples to be cured. In verse 18, Jesus cast the demon out of the boy, and he was cured.

2. Is this account suggesting epilepsy, even epilepsy today, is caused by evil spirits?

(Note: Most people will say that epilepsy is a physical condition caused by a breakdown in a biological process even though we do not fully understand the breakdown. Some will say that, perhaps in this unique case, a demon was causing the epilepsy, but that does not imply that all epileptics are demon possessed.)

3. In Mark 9:22, the father says to Jesus, "If you can do anything . . ." What did that statement reveal about the father's belief?

The father obviously did not fully believe. He believed enough to bring his son to the disciples and to Jesus, but the word "if" implies doubt.

4. Jesus instructed the father that if he believes, all things are possible. Do you agree with that statement?

5. What was the father saying when he said, "I believe, help my unbelief"?

The father was acknowledging that he wanted to believe. Many people today want to believe but do not fully believe. If you ask them if there is a God, they say, "yes." If you ask them if Jesus is the Son of God, they say, "yes." If you ask them if they believe in heaven and hell and Judgment Day, they say, "maybe." If you ask them if they are going to heaven, they look down and say, "I hope so." These people have an incomplete faith, just like the father who brought his epileptic son to Jesus. They want to believe but don't really believe.

6. Should people pray for God to "help them with their unbelief"? Will God help strengthen people's belief?

God will sometimes strengthen people's belief, but it usually comes through great trials. If you pray that your faith be strengthened, be prepared for trials.

Mark 9:30–32

> [30]They went out from there, and passed through Galilee. He didn't want anyone to know it. [31]For he was teaching his disciples, and said to them, "The Son of Man is being handed over to the hands of men, and they will kill him; and when he is killed, on the third day he will rise again."

> [32]But they didn't understand the saying, and were afraid to ask him.

1. This is the second time Jesus told the disciples that the Son of Man is going to be killed but will rise on the third day. Why can't they understand what he is saying?

They believed that Jesus was the Messiah, but they also believed that the Messiah was going to defeat the Romans and become king. To them, Messiah does not die. They had preconceived ideas that prevented them from understanding the truth.

Mark 9:33-50

[33]He came to Capernaum, and when he was in the house he asked them, "What were you arguing among yourselves on the way?"

[34]But they were silent, for they had disputed one with another on the way about who was the greatest.

[35]He sat down, and called the twelve; and he said to them, "If any man wants to be first, he shall be last of all, and servant of all." [36]He took a little child, and set him in their midst. Taking him in his arms, he said to them, [37]"Whoever receives one such little child in my name, receives me, and whoever receives me, doesn't receive me, but him who sent me."

[38]John said to him, "Teacher, we saw someone who doesn't follow us casting out demons in your name; and we forbade him, because he doesn't follow us."

[39]But Jesus said, "Don't forbid him, for there is no one who will do a mighty work in my name, and be able quickly to speak evil of me. [40]For whoever is not against us is on our side. [41]For whoever will give you a cup of water to drink in my name, because you are Christ's, most certainly I tell you, he will in no way lose his reward. [42]Whoever will cause one of these little ones who believe in me to stumble, it would be better for him if he were thrown into the sea with a millstone hung around his neck. [43]If your hand causes you to stumble, cut it off. It is better for you to enter into life maimed, rather than having your two hands to go into Gehenna,[48] into the unquenchable fire, [44]'where their worm doesn't die, and the fire is not quenched.' [45]If your foot causes you to stumble, cut it off. It is better for you to enter into life lame, rather than having your two feet to be cast into Gehenna,[49] into the fire that will never be quenched—[46]'where their worm doesn't die, and the fire is not quenched.' [47]If your eye causes you to stumble, cast it out. It is better

---

[48]   9:43 or, Hell
[49]   9:45 or, Hell

for you to enter into the kingdom of God with one eye, rather than having two eyes to be cast into the Gehenna[50] of fire, [48]'where their worm doesn't die, and the fire is not quenched.'[51] [49]For everyone will be salted with fire, and every sacrifice will be seasoned with salt. [50]Salt is good, but if the salt has lost its saltiness, with what will you season it? Have salt in yourselves, and be at peace with one another."

(Note: This is actually one section literarily governed by the themes of arguing with one another with a little child in front of them.)

1. What were the disciples doing immediately after Jesus predicted his death?

They were arguing about who was the greatest among them.

2. What did Jesus say about being the greatest?

If you want to be first, be last and the servant of all. Then he held a little child in his arms and said that receiving a little child is like receiving Jesus.

This is the second death prediction. This is the second time Jesus explained what it meant to be the Messiah. He followed the explanation with what it meant to be a disciple. It means becoming the least and the servant of all.

A little child is the least respected in Jewish culture. Instead of claiming to be in charge, a little child does what the adults say. The followers of Jesus who want to be first need to be last and servants to everyone, like children.

3. In verse 38, John said there was a man casting out demons in Jesus' name, and they told him to stop because he did not

---

follow Jesus and the disciples. How does this fit in with the teaching that whoever wants to be first must be last?

The disciples were upset because this man was not following Jesus as part of their fellowship or organization. Jesus taught that if the man is doing good in Jesus' name, do not stop him.

One of the greatest hindrances to unbelievers today is denominationalism and the fractured nature of the church. Some denominations claim that you have to be in their fellowship to be saved. Jesus says that anyone doing good in his name should be allowed to do so. If anyone gives a cup of water (a small gesture of support) to the disciples because they are working for Jesus, that person will not lose their reward. People who do good in the name of Jesus but are not in your denomination are not necessarily excluded from the kingdom, and their work must not be stopped.

4. **In verse 42, Jesus returned to the concept of "little ones." Was he talking about children who believe or people who are not part of their fellowship?**

Both. Jesus said causing anyone to stumble in their belief is a major issue.

5. **Jesus expounded on the idea that people or things can cause stumbling and said that if any part of your body caused you to sin, cut it off. It is better to live without that body part than to sin and go to hell. Was Jesus advocating self-mutilation?**

Jesus was illustrating that sin is more serious and devastating than losing body parts. Jesus was not advocating that people deal with sin through mutilation. If someone is addicted to porn, the problem is not in their eyes, and blinding them will not change their heart. In the Sermon on the Mount, Jesus taught that true righteousness requires a change of heart. A change of heart takes place by accepting a new Spirit. Righteousness by faith and spirit are core concepts of Christianity and no one advocates self-mutilation as an effective way to deal with sin.

6. Jesus speaks of hell several times. Does hell exist? Could a loving God really send people to a place of torment for all eternity?

The question is not, "Could a loving God send people to hell?" The question is, "Could a loving God NOT send people to hell?" It is much like the philosophical question of evil: "If God is all-loving, he would be motivated to end suffering. If God is all-powerful, he possesses the power to end suffering. Therefore, God is either not all-loving or not all-powerful." The question of evil assumes that this life is supposed to be fair.

This life is unfair. There is cancer, MS, ALS, leukemia, and millions of babies, children, and young people are dying. There is rape, murder, incest, stealing, human trafficking, etc. There is evil in the world.

The point is this: The evil in the world is the best evidence of the existence of heaven and hell. The only way to make this life fair is through an afterlife where we reap the consequences of our actions without fail.

The only way for a child who died of leukemia to have any fairness is if he or she can live a new life with no disease.

This world is only the proving ground where our eternity is formed.

7. What did Jesus mean when he said you should have salt in yourself and be at peace with one another?

Jesus said they would be salted with fire, which meant they would be tested. He also said their sacrifices would be seasoned with salt, which was the Jewish custom in offering sacrifices (Leviticus 2:13). He was saying they would all be tested and persecuted, (salted) and they should view their persecutions as salting that makes the sacrifice acceptable to God. Having salt in yourselves, or among yourselves, was a Jewish way of saying they should be in fellowship with each other. In their culture, food was scarce, and this affected their levels of relationship. They had relatives and friends, who they would share a meal with, and acquaintances, who they would not invite to their table. People who you shared salt with were said to share a covenant of salt (2 Chronicles 13:5).

Jesus said that they would all be tested and persecuted and a common experience of persecution should cause them to bond together and protect each other. He said they should have salt among each other, or be in table fellowship, and share in a covenant of salt; they should be at peace with each other. He said this as a conclusion to his comments because they had been arguing with each other on the road about who was the greatest.

Chapter 10

Mark 10:1-12

[1]He arose from there and came into the borders of Judea and beyond the Jordan. Multitudes came together to him again. As he usually did, he was again teaching them. [2]Pharisees came to him testing him, and asked him, "Is it lawful for a man to divorce his wife?"

[3]He answered, "What did Moses command you?"

[4]They said, "Moses allowed a certificate of divorce to be written, and to divorce her."

[5]But Jesus said to them, "For your hardness of heart, he wrote you this commandment. [6]But from the beginning of the creation, God made them male and female.[52] [7]For this cause a man will leave his father and mother, and will join to his wife, [8]and the two will become one flesh,[53] so that they are no longer two, but one flesh. [9]What therefore God has joined together, let no man separate."

[10]In the house, his disciples asked him again about the same matter. [11]He said to them, "Whoever divorces his wife, and marries another, commits adultery against her. [12]If a woman herself divorces her husband, and marries another, she commits adultery."

---

[52]   10:6 Genesis 1:27
[53]   10:8 Genesis 2:24

1. Why did the Pharisees test Jesus?

They wanted to discredit him in front of the people. They were jealous that the people loved Jesus and wanted to follow his teachings instead of them. They were threatened by the talk of making Jesus king and causing a revolution and revolt against Rome. Too much talk of revolt would bring the wrath of Rome against all of them.

2. Why did the Pharisees use a question about divorce to test Jesus?

Divorce was a hot topic in their time. There were two schools of thought about divorce among rabbis. The different perspectives came from different interpretations of Deuteronomy 24:1-4.

Deuteronomy 24:1-4

> [1]When a man takes a wife, and marries her, then it shall be, if she find no favor in his eyes, because he has found some unseemly thing in her, that he shall write her a bill of divorce, and give it in her hand, and send her out of his house. [2]When she is departed out of his house, she may go and be another man's wife. [3]If the latter husband hate her, and write her a bill of divorce, and give it in her hand, and send her out of his house; or if the latter husband die, who took her to be his wife; [4]her former husband, who sent her away, may not take her again to be his wife, after that she is defiled; for that is abomination before the Lord: and you shall not cause the land to sin, which the Lord your God gives you for an inheritance.

The arguments centered on the interpretation of the first verse: "because he has found some unseemly thing in her." What was a justifiable reason for divorce? A famous rabbi, named Shammai, taught that unseemly meant adultery and only adultery. The school of Shammai taught that the only reason a man could divorce his wife was for marital unfaithfulness.

Another famous rabbi, Hillel, gave the widest possible interpretation and taught that anything displeasing to the husband could be grounds for divorce.

The Pharisees were testing Jesus by asking whether he followed the school of Shammai or the school of Hillel on this hot topic. Jesus said he followed the school of God by quoting Genesis 1:27 and 2:24. God intended marriage to be permanent. Marriage is between a man and a woman and when they take vows to be faithful to each other and love, honor, and cherish each other, they form a marriage covenant that is not to be broken and no man should divide what God has combined.

Matthew 19:1-12

[1]It happened when Jesus had finished these words, he departed from Galilee, and came into the borders of Judea beyond the Jordan. [2]Great multitudes followed him, and he healed them there. [3]Pharisees came to him, testing him, and saying, "Is it lawful for a man to divorce his wife for any reason?"

[4]He answered, "Haven't you read that he who made them from the beginning made them male and female,[54] [5]and said, 'For this cause a man shall leave his father and mother, and shall join to his wife; and the two shall become one flesh?'[55] [6]So that they are no more two, but one flesh. What therefore God has joined together, don't let man tear apart."

[7]They asked him, "Why then did Moses command us to give her a bill of divorce, and divorce her?"

[8]He said to them, "Moses, because of the hardness of your hearts, allowed you to divorce your wives, but from the beginning it has not been so. [9]I tell you that whoever divorces his wife, except for sexual immorality, and marries another, commits adultery; and he who marries her when she is divorced commits adultery."

[10]His disciples said to him, "If this is the case of the man with his wife, it is not expedient to marry."

---

[54] 19:4 Genesis 1:27
[55] 19:5 Genesis 2:24

[11]But he said to them, "Not all men can receive this saying, but those to whom it is given. [12]For there are eunuchs who were born that way from their mother's womb, and there are eunuchs who were made eunuchs by men; and there are eunuchs who made themselves eunuchs for the kingdom of Heaven's sake. He who is able to receive it, let him receive it."

Matthew records an important detail that Mark omitted. Matthew records Jesus saying sexual immorality (or adultery) is the only reason for divorce. Although Mark does not explicitly include that, it is implied from the arguments.

Here are the points. Marriage is a sacred commitment between a man and a woman that forms a marriage covenant for life. It can only be broken by adultery. The certificate of divorce that Moses allowed was intended to allow the woman to remarry legally. If a man divorces his wife for some reason other than adultery and marries another woman, he commits adultery.

Most people today do not have a problem with the concept that marriage is for life. They have a problem with various teachings about repentance after a divorce.

Some denominations teach that you can be forgiven if you divorce and remarry. Other denominations teach that if a divorced man marries another woman, he is living in adultery. They argue that such a man must repent of adultery to be forgiven. To repent, these denominations say the man must divorce his new wife and live alone. Much like legalistic Pharisees, their requirement to be righteous would break up a functioning family for the sake of religious teaching. If your conclusion violates the original command of God that marriage should not be dissolved, something is wrong with your interpretation.

The question then becomes what is repentance for someone married to a second or subsequent spouse? Is it to choose to live a committed, life-long relationship with the new spouse? Or, is it to break up a functioning marriage?

To summarize, Jesus said in Matthew 19:11 that not all people could follow this teaching. He clearly states that some men choose celibacy for the kingdom of heaven but not everyone could, or should, do that. Not everyone can follow the teaching on marriage. Is it a sin to break up a marriage for reasons other than adultery? According to Jesus' teaching, it is. The apostle Paul, however, did allow divorce between a believer and an unbeliever if the unbeliever chose to leave the marriage (1 Corinthians 7:15). But divorce and remarriage is not the unforgivable sin. Repentance is choosing to agree with God's teaching that a man should leave his father and mother and hold to his wife, and the two should be committed to each other for life. Repentance is not breaking up more marriages. That would violate the very command it is intended to enforce.

If a man or woman divorces and remarries, they can repent, commit, live in a godly marriage relationship, and be forgiven.

Mark 10:17-31

[17]As he was going out into the way, one ran to him, knelt before him, and asked him, "Good Teacher, what shall I do that I may inherit eternal life?"

[18]Jesus said to him, "Why do you call me good? No one is good except one—God. [19]You know the commandments: 'Do not murder,' 'Do not commit adultery,' 'Do not steal,' 'Do not give false testimony,' 'Do not defraud,' 'Honor your father and mother.'"[56]

[20]He said to him, "Teacher, I have observed all these things from my youth."

[21]Jesus looking at him loved him, and said to him, "One thing you lack. Go, sell whatever you have, and give to the poor, and you will have treasure in heaven; and come, follow me, taking up the cross."

---

[56]   10:19 Exodus 20:12–16; Deuteronomy 5:16–20

[22]But his face fell at that saying, and he went away sorrowful, for he was one who had great possessions. [23]Jesus looked around, and said to his disciples, "How difficult it is for those who have riches to enter into the kingdom of God!"

[24]The disciples were amazed at his words. But Jesus answered again, "Children, how hard is it for those who trust in riches to enter into the kingdom of God! [25]It is easier for a camel to go through a needle's eye than for a rich man to enter into the kingdom of God."

[26]They were exceedingly astonished, saying to him, "Then who can be saved?"

[27]Jesus, looking at them, said, "With men it is impossible, but not with God, for all things are possible with God."

[28]Peter began to tell him, "Behold, we have left all, and have followed you."

[29]Jesus said, "Most certainly I tell you, there is no one who has left house, or brothers, or sisters, or father, or mother, or wife, or children, or land, for my sake, and for the sake of the gospel, [30]but he will receive one hundred times more now in this time, houses, brothers, sisters, mothers, children, and land, with persecutions; and in the age to come eternal life. [31]But many who are first will be last; and the last first."

1. Why did Jesus question being called good?

The rich man thought he was good. He claimed to have kept most of the Ten Commandments since youth. Jesus challenged this concept by reminding him that no one is good except God. Of course, there is a double meaning here because it also implies that if Jesus is good, he is God.

2. Why did Jesus tell this man to sell all his possessions? Is that a requirement for salvation?

The man was asking if there was something more he could do to ensure his salvation. Keeping the commandments did not appear to be a problem for this man, except that he was breaking the very first commandment, "You shall have no other gods before me" (Exodus 20:3).

Anything we worship more than God is a problem. Jesus said in Matthew 6:24, "No one can serve two masters, for either he will hate the one and love the other; or else he will be devoted to one and despise the other. You can't serve both God and Mammon."

This man was breaking the very first commandment but claiming to keep the others. He was self-deceived.

3. Are people self-deceived today?

Some people think they will get into heaven because they attend church once in a while. Other people think they will get into heaven because they give to a charity or serve in a soup kitchen.

Some people, like this rich man, think they are better than others; therefore, they deserve to go to heaven. They say, "I'm not like those drug addicts or gang members, I'm a good person."

Jesus taught that it is impossible for any of us to get into heaven based on being good enough. Only by being in Christ and covered by the sacrifice of Jesus on the cross can we be redeemed.

4. Jesus said it is easier for a camel to go through the eye of a needle than for a rich man to get into heaven. Why were the disciples astonished by this?

The disciples knew that Jesus was saying it was impossible for a rich man to go to heaven. Many interesting theories have been suggested to mitigate the meaning and lessen the impact of this teaching. One theory, from the 1500s, suggested there was a small gate in the wall of Jerusalem called "the needle" and a camel had to be unloaded of its burdens to fit through the gate. There is no historical evidence of such a gate. Another theory, published by Dr. George M. Lamsa, suggests that since Jesus and the disciples spoke Aramaic, Jesus would have used the Aramaic word "gamla," which meant either camel or rope, depending on context.[57] Dr. Lamsa suggests the verse should read, "it would be easier for a rope to go through the eye of a needle than for a rich man to go to heaven." Whichever theory you ascribe to, the disciples were astonished because Jesus was saying you cannot worship and serve money over God and still go to heaven.

Mark 10:32-34

[32]They were on the way, going up to Jerusalem; and Jesus was going in front of them, and they were amazed; and those who followed were afraid. He again took the twelve, and began to tell them the things that were going to happen to him. [33]"Behold, we are going up to Jerusalem. The Son of Man will be delivered to the chief priests and the scribes. They will condemn him to death, and will deliver him to the Gentiles. [34]They will mock him, spit on him, scourge him, and kill him. On the third day he will rise again."

1. **This is the third time Jesus predicted his death and resurrection. This time he is on his way to Jerusalem. What do you imagine the disciples are thinking?**

This time they are headed toward Jerusalem, so the idea that Jesus might be handed over to the Gentiles (Romans) seemed like a potentially real option. It says they were afraid. Maybe they are beginning to listen to him.

2. **Does the fact that Jesus predicted future events in detail mean anything?**

Yes, accurately foretelling the future is evidence that he really is the Son of God.

---

[57]   Lamsa, George, M., Gospel Light, (A. J. Holman Co., 1939)

Mark 10:35-45

³⁵James and John, the sons of Zebedee, came near to him, saying, "Teacher, we want you to do for us whatever we will ask."

³⁶He said to them, "What do you want me to do for you?"

³⁷They said to him, "Grant to us that we may sit, one at your right hand, and one at your left hand, in your glory."

³⁸But Jesus said to them, "You don't know what you are asking. Are you able to drink the cup that I drink, and to be baptized with the baptism that I am baptized with?"

³⁹They said to him, "We are able."

Jesus said to them, "You shall indeed drink the cup that I drink, and you shall be baptized with the baptism that I am baptized with; ⁴⁰but to sit at my right hand and at my left hand is not mine to give, but for whom it has been prepared."

⁴¹When the ten heard it, they began to be indignant towards James and John.

⁴²Jesus summoned them, and said to them, "You know that they who are recognized as rulers over the nations lord it over them, and their great ones exercise authority over them. ⁴³But it shall not be so among you, but whoever wants to become great among you shall be your servant. ⁴⁴Whoever of you wants to become first among you, shall be bondservant of all. ⁴⁵For the Son of Man also came not to be served, but to serve, and to give his life as a ransom for many."

1. What did James and John ask for?

They still expected Jesus to be an earthly king. To them, the phrase "in your glory" meant glory as a king. We know that Jesus came into his glory and sat at the right hand of God in heaven and rules as King of Kings and Lord of Lords. James and John did not know about that. They thought Jesus was going to be an earthly king, and they were asking for the highest levels of power in his administration. Jesus told them plainly that they did not know what they were asking for.

2. What did Jesus mean when he asked them, "Are you able to drink the cup that I drink, and to be baptized with the baptism that I am baptized with?"?

In Mark 14:36, when Jesus was in the Garden of Gethsemane praying, he asked the Father "to take this cup from me." It was a figurative reference to the betrayal, rejection, beatings, humiliation, and crucifixion that was about to happen. Baptism is used in the same figurative way.

Jesus is rhetorically asking James and John if they can drink the cup he is about to drink. In other words, "Are you able to go through what I am about to go through?" Sharing in this "cup" has strong associations to communion, where all followers of Jesus share in the life of Jesus, the love, and the persecutions.

There is an idiom about "baptism by fire" that means going through events that test a person. It is not a literal, ritualistic baptism with fire, but events that test one's soul. In this case, Jesus is using baptism to refer to the crucifixion. Romans 6:3-4 relates baptism to the crucifixion, burial and resurrection.

Romans 6:3-4

> [3]Or don't you know that all we who were baptized into Christ Jesus were baptized into his death? [4]We were buried therefore with him through baptism to death, that just like Christ was raised from the dead through the glory of the Father, so we also might walk in newness of life.

When a person dies to their evil self, is buried in water, and brought back up out of the water to live a new life as a follower of Jesus, they are symbolically sharing in the death, burial, and resurrection of Jesus.

James and John answered that they could share in the cup and the baptism. They had no idea what they were saying. Jesus affirmed that they would actually share in his experiences. Acts 12:2 tells us that

James suffered martyrdom at the hands of Herod about ten years after the crucifixion. John went through many persecutions up to exile on the Island of Patmos (Revelation 1:9).

3. Why were the ten indignant?

They also wanted to be the greatest and most powerful. They saw James and John making a play for power.

4. What did Jesus teach in response to this power play?

Verses 42 through 45 are the third teachings on what it means to be a follower of Jesus. The kingdom is different than the world. In the kingdom of God, the greatest are the servants. Greatness comes through serving, not commanding.

Mark 10:46-52

> [46]They came to Jericho. As he went out from Jericho, with his disciples and a great multitude, the son of Timaeus, Bartimaeus, a blind beggar, was sitting by the road. [47]When he heard that it was Jesus the Nazarene, he began to cry out, and say, "Jesus, you son of David, have mercy on me!" [48]Many rebuked him, that he should be quiet, but he cried out much more, "You son of David, have mercy on me!"

> [49]Jesus stood still, and said, "Call him."

> They called the blind man, saying to him, "Cheer up! Get up. He is calling you!"

> [50]He, casting away his cloak, sprang up, and came to Jesus.

> [51]Jesus asked him, "What do you want me to do for you?"

> The blind man said to him, "Rabboni,[58] that I may see again."

---

[58] 10:51 Rabboni is a transliteration of the Hebrew word for "great teacher."

[52]Jesus said to him, "Go your way. Your faith has made you well." Immediately he received his sight, and followed Jesus in the way.

1. What does the blind man's persistence and refusal to be quiet teach us?

God listens to those who pray over and over and will not stop praying. Luke 18:1-8 is a parable about a persistent woman who petitions a judge over and over until she gets justice. This blind man would not be silenced. His persistence gained him an audience with Jesus.

2. What was the significance of the blind man calling Jesus "you son of David"?

Part of the Messianic teaching and expectation of the time was that the Messiah would be a descendant of David. Matthew 1:6 and Luke 3:31 clearly demonstrate that Jesus was a descendant of—David—at least in his earthly lineage. The blind man was purposely calling Jesus by a Messianic title.

3. What happened the last time Jesus healed a blind man?

In Mark 8:22-26, Jesus deliberately took two tries to heal a blind man to make a point. Here, Jesus healed the blind man by simply speaking the words. These two accounts form bookends, or markers, of a major section in the book of Mark.

4. How would you feel if you were blind and Jesus healed you?

In a way, the blind man in this story represents us. We were blind but the teaching of Jesus heals us and lets us see the truth about life, the world, and ourselves.

Chapter 11

¹When they drew near to Jerusalem, to Bethsphage[59] and Bethany, at the Mount of Olives, he sent two of his disciples, ²and said to them, "Go your way into the village that is opposite you. Immediatcly as you enter into it, you will find a young donkey tied, on which no one has sat. Untie him, and bring him. ³If anyone asks you, 'Why are you doing this?' say, 'the Lord needs him;' and immediately he will send him back here."

⁴They went away, and found a young donkey tied at the door outside in the open street, and they untied him. ⁵Some of those who stood there asked them, "What are you doing, untying the young donkey?" ⁶They said to them just as Jesus had said, and they let them go.

⁷They brought the young donkey to Jesus, and threw their garments on it, and Jesus sat on it. ⁸Many spread their garments on the way, and others were cutting down branches from the trees, and spreading them on the road. ⁹Those who went in front, and those who followed, cried out, "Hosanna[60]! Blessed is he who comes in the name of the Lord![61] ¹⁰Blessed is the kingdom of our father

---

[59]   11:1 TR & NU read "Bethphage" instead of "Bethsphage."
[60]   11:9 "Hosanna" means "save us" or "help us, we pray."
[61]   11:9 Psalm 118:25-26

David that is coming in the name of the Lord! Hosanna in the highest!"

¹¹Jesus entered into the temple in Jerusalem. When he had looked around at everything, it being now evening, he went out to Bethany with the twelve.

(Note: The Triumphal Entry is generally believed to have occurred on the Sunday before the crucifixion and resurrection the following Friday and Sunday. About a third of Mark, from Mark 11 to the end of the book, is devoted to this last week, commonly referred to as the Passion Week.)

1. **Why a young donkey? Would it have been more kingly to ride in on a powerful stallion?**

Zechariah 9:9-10

> ⁹Rejoice greatly, daughter of Zion!
>   Shout, daughter of Jerusalem!
> Behold, your King comes to you!
>   He is righteous, and having salvation;
>   lowly, and riding on a donkey,
>   even on a colt, the foal of a donkey.
> ¹⁰I will cut off the chariot from Ephraim,
>   and the horse from Jerusalem;
> and the battle bow will be cut off;
>   and he will speak peace to the nations:
>   and his dominion will be from sea to sea,
>   and from the River to the ends of the earth.

This ride into Jerusalem was to fulfill the prophecy in Zechariah, which the Jews knew well and talked about often. Mark 11:10 shows how much the people expected the immediate coming of the kingdom. Jesus knew that riding a young donkey into Jerusalem would declare that he was the Messiah. This is a distinct change from all the times up to this point that Jesus tells people to be quiet.

Revelation 19:11–16

[11]I saw the heaven opened, and behold, a white horse, and he who sat on it is called Faithful and True. In righteousness he judges and makes war. [12]His eyes are a flame of fire, and on his head are many crowns. He has names written and a name written which no one knows but he himself. [13]He is clothed in a garment sprinkled with blood. His name is called "The Word of God." [14]The armies which are in heaven followed him on white horses, clothed in white, pure, fine linen. [15]Out of his mouth proceeds a sharp, double-edged sword, that with it he should strike the nations. He will rule them with an iron rod.[62] He treads the winepress of the fierceness of the wrath of God, the Almighty. [16]He has on his garment and on his thigh a name written, "KING OF KINGS, AND LORD OF LORDS."

The book of Revelation presents spiritual truths in symbolic language. In this symbolism, Jesus returns riding a white horse to judge and make war. This is the picture John paints of the judging Jesus.

The Messianic Jesus riding into Jerusalem on a young donkey is a picture of humility. Riding on a donkey, instead of a war horse, suggested he came to bring peace.

2. How did Jesus know there would be a colt or young donkey waiting?

The most probable answer is that he is Jesus, the Son of God. Just as he knew about the coming betrayal, scourging, crucifixion, and resurrection, he had foreknowledge of the young donkey.

The Jewish people knew and talked about the prophecy in Zechariah 9. Perhaps a breeder always kept a young donkey near the gate hoping that the Messiah would come. The people of the area would have known what the donkey, waiting in the same location every day, meant. Verse 5 says, "Some of those who stood there asked them, 'What are you

---

[62]   19:15 Psalm 2:9

doing, untying the young donkey?'" It did not say the owner asked the question. The people, knowing what the donkey was for, were curious. When the disciples said, "the Lord needs it," the people understood that the disciples were saying, "The Messiah needs it."

3. Would you let someone borrow your car if "the Lord needed it"?

Yes, but the real question becomes "what would you hold back and refuse to give in service to God?"

Mark 11:12-14

[12]The next day, when they had come out from Bethany, he was hungry. [13]Seeing a fig tree afar off having leaves, he came to see if perhaps he might find anything on it. When he came to it, he found nothing but leaves, for it was not the season for figs. [14]Jesus told it, "May no one ever eat fruit from you again!" and his disciples heard it.

1. Does this seem harsh compared to your mental image of Jesus?

There is a good reason for the curse, which will be discussed in Mark 11:20-26.

Mark 11:15-19

[15]They came to Jerusalem, and Jesus entered into the temple, and began to throw out those who sold and those who bought in the temple, and overthrew the tables of the money changers, and the seats of those who sold the doves. [16]He would not allow anyone to carry a container through the temple. [17]He taught, saying to them, "Isn't it written, 'My house will be called a house of prayer for all the nations?'[63] But you have made it a den of robbers!"[64]

---

[63]   11:17 Isaiah 56:7
[64]   11:17 Jeremiah 7:11

[18]The chief priests and the scribes heard it, and sought how they might destroy him. For they feared him, because all the multitude was astonished at his teaching.

[19]When evening came, he went out of the city.

1. Did Jesus get angry? Was it a sin?

Ephesians 4:26-27

[26]"Be angry, and don't sin."[65] Don't let the sun go down on your wrath, [27]neither give place to the devil.

The Bible says people get angry. Numerous verses cite the wrath of God. It is not a sin to be angry, especially if it is over a just cause. But anger can lead to sinful actions. Anger must be controlled, and we cannot let anger make us say or do things that are sin.

2. Why was Jesus so angry?

The Jewish temple was the heart of the Jewish religion. If there was corruption in the temple, it was corrupt through and through. The design of the temple had multiple courts or courtyards for various groups of people. There was the Court of the Priests, where only priests could go. There was the Court of the Israelites, the Court of Women, and, finally, the Court of the Gentiles.

Isaiah 56:6-7

[6]Also the foreigners who join themselves to the Lord, to minister to him, and to love the name of the Lord, to be his servants, everyone who keeps the Sabbath from profaning it, and holds fast my covenant; [7]even them will I bring to my holy mountain, and make them joyful in my house of prayer: their burnt offerings and their sacrifices shall be accepted on my altar; for my house shall be called a house of prayer for all peoples."

---

[65]   4:26 Psalm 4:4

Jesus quoted part of this verse to remind the Jewish religious leaders that the Court of the Gentiles was ordained in the Bible. The Jewish leaders took the Court of the Gentiles and filled it with money changers and animals sold for sacrifices. Annas, the high priest, had quite a business. The priests had to be descendants from the tribe of Levi. That meant all the priests working in the temple were related in some manner.

The Israelites were required to pay a temple tax in a certain currency. The Jews who traveled from far away had to exchange their currency, and the rates were unfair.

The priests also sold animals for sacrifice in the Court of the Gentiles. Although a worshipper could buy an animal outside the temple for half the price of the animals in the temple, the priests would reject the animal from outside as blemished. Annas and the priests were getting rich.

Jesus put a stop to the practice. This is another reason they wanted to kill him.

Mark 11:20-26

[20]As they passed by in the morning, they saw the fig tree withered away from the roots. [21]Peter, remembering, said to him, "Rabbi, look! The fig tree which you cursed has withered away."

[22]Jesus answered them, "Have faith in God. [23]For most certainly I tell you, whoever may tell this mountain, 'Be taken up and cast into the sea,' and doesn't doubt in his heart, but believes that what he says is happening; he shall have whatever he says. [24]Therefore I tell you, all things whatever you pray and ask for, believe that you have received them, and you shall have them. [25]Whenever you stand praying, forgive, if you have anything against anyone; so that your Father, who is in heaven, may also forgive you your transgressions. [26]But if you do not forgive, neither will your Father in heaven forgive your transgressions."

1. **This is the other half of the story about the fig tree. Do you think there is a reason the cleansing of the temple was inserted between the beginning and end of the fig tree story?**

The fig tree represented Israel and, specifically, the religion of Israel. Because of the hardness of their hearts and refusal to accept Jesus, they are like a fig tree that bears no fruit. Their fruitlessness in the sight of God will lead to a curse. The religious leaders, the Chief Priest, scribes, and Pharisees, are the root of the Jewish religion, but this is a tree that will wither from the root because the root has become corrupt.

2. **Why did Jesus tell the disciples to "have faith in God," and what did he mean?**

The disciples were surprised that the fig tree withered. After seeing all the miracles that Jesus did, it seems odd that they were surprised Jesus could wither a tree with a curse. It may be they were more surprised that Jesus did wither a tree, especially at a time of year when there was not supposed to be any fruit on it. Jesus' answer seems to address their surprise instead of his motivation.

Jesus taught them that belief can move mountains. He taught them that if you truly believe and do not doubt, you can have whatever you ask for. The secret is to believe you have already received what you asked for.

3. **Do you believe this?**

(Interesting discussions will ensue.)

4. **What if you pray, believing without a doubt and believing you have already received what you asked for, but what you asked for is contrary to God's will because it would be destructive to you to have it?**

It is good that God will not give us everything we ask for.

5. **Why did Jesus teach about forgiveness in a lesson about faith and prayer?**

This is an illustration. If you ask God to forgive you but you will not forgive others, God will not forgive you. Similarly, if you forgive others, God will forgive you.

Most people stop there and miss the point. This teaching is not limited to forgiveness. Forgiveness is merely one example to illustrate a larger principle.

If you pray and ask God to give you money, do you give money to those who ask you for money? His point is that if you will not give to others, God will not give to you.

If you pray and ask God for help, do you help others? If you refuse to help others, God refuses to help you.

Forgiveness is taught in the context of faith and withering fig trees or moving mountains. Jesus is saying, "If you ask God to move a mountain for you, are you going to help others move mountains too?"

6. Why is it essential to forgive?

People hurt each other intentionally and unintentionally. It is a fact of life. All relationships, especially marriage relationships, die without forgiveness.

Imagine a married couple, Henry and Martha. Henry says some things in front of friends at a party that embarrasses Martha. Martha feels resentment, betrayal, and a loss of trust because her best friend, her partner, her lover, and husband hurt her. Martha thinks that if she chooses to forgive with no expectation that Henry will change his behavior, she will feel like a door mat and compromise her dignity and self-esteem.

Here is what should happen. Henry realizes what he did and says, "I am sorry. I spoke without thinking about how it would affect you, and I am terribly sorry I hurt you. It will not happen again because the last thing I want to do is hurt you. Please forgive me." Saying, "I am sorry" means, "I realize how I offended you and commit to not do it again." There are three things that have to occur. First, there needs to be genuine recognition that the offense occurred. Henry needs to realize and acknowledge that Martha was hurt, so Martha knows that Henry agrees that the offense was wrong. Second, Henry needs to understand that trust has been lost. Henry needs to repent and promise never to repeat the offense. This restores trust to some extent but needs to be followed with actions that will continue to build trust. Third, Henry needs to ask for forgiveness. "Please forgive me" is asking to restore the relationship to the way it was before the offense.

Forgiveness has the potential to restore relationships if done under the right circumstances. Forgiving under the wrong circumstances can add to the offense by diminishing ourselves and making us feel like door mats.

Matthew 18:21–35

[21]Then Peter came and said to him, "Lord, how often shall my brother sin against me, and I forgive him? Until seven times?"

[22]Jesus said to him, "I don't tell you until seven times, but, until seventy times seven. [23]Therefore the kingdom of Heaven is like a certain king, who wanted to reconcile accounts with his servants. [24]When he had begun to reconcile, one was brought to him who owed him ten thousand talents.[66] [25]But because he couldn't pay, his lord commanded him to be sold, with his wife, his children, and all that he had, and payment to be made. [26]The servant therefore fell down and kneeled before him, saying, 'Lord, have patience with me, and I will repay you all!' [27]The lord of that servant, being moved with compassion, released him, and forgave him the debt.

[28]"But that servant went out, and found one of his fellow servants, who owed him one hundred denarii,[67] and he grabbed him, and took him by the throat, saying, 'Pay me what you owe!'

---

[66] 18:24 Ten thousand talents represents an extremely large sum of money, equivalent to about 60,000,000 denarii, where one denarius was typical of one day's wages for agricultural labor.

[67] 18:28 100 denarii was about one sixtieth of a talent.

²⁹"So his fellow servant fell down at his feet and begged him, saying, 'Have patience with me, and I will repay you!' ³⁰He would not, but went and cast him into prison, until he should pay back that which was due. ³¹So when his fellow servants saw what was done, they were exceedingly sorry, and came and told to their lord all that was done. ³²Then his lord called him in, and said to him, 'You wicked servant! I forgave you all that debt, because you begged me. ³³Shouldn't you also have had mercy on your fellow servant, even as I had mercy on you?' ³⁴His lord was angry, and delivered him to the tormentors, until he should pay all that was due to him. ³⁵So my heavenly Father will also do to you, if you don't each forgive your brother from your hearts for his misdeeds."

Peter specifically asked whether we have a duty to forgive. Jesus said we must forgive as often as someone sincerely asks for our forgiveness. We must forgive because we have been forgiven of a debt 600,000 times greater than anything owed to us.

Mark 11:27-33

²⁷They came again to Jerusalem, and as he was walking in the temple, the chief priests, and the scribes, and the elders came to him, ²⁸and they began saying to him, "By what authority do you do these things? Or who gave you this authority to do these things?"

²⁹Jesus said to them, "I will ask you one question. Answer me, and I will tell you by what authority I do these things. ³⁰The baptism of John—was it from heaven, or from men? Answer me."

³¹They reasoned with themselves, saying, "If we should say, 'From heaven;' he will say, 'Why then did you not believe him?' ³²If we should say, 'From men'"—they feared the people, for all held John to really be a prophet. ³³They answered Jesus, "We don't know."

Jesus said to them, "Neither do I tell you by what authority I do these things."

(Note: Mark 11:27 through Mark 12 is a section of testing. The chief priests, scribes and elders [11:27], Pharisees and Herodians [12:13], Sadducees [12:18] *and, finally, another scribe [12:28] each took a turn testing Jesus. When religion could not discredit Jesus, they realized they were actually increasing his popularity among the people. This section ends with Jesus blasting the religious leaders for making a show of giving and contrasting them with a poor widow, who Jesus said was far greater than them.)*

1. **What were the religious leaders asking Jesus when they asked, "By what authority do you do these things?" What were "these things?"**

Riding into Jerusalem on a donkey, teaching against them, clearing the Temple, etc.

2. **Why did Jesus refuse to tell them?**

They would not accept anything he said. Their minds were made up. They wanted to believe what they wanted to believe and no amount of reason could change it.

Romans 1:18-32

[18]For the wrath of God is revealed from heaven against all ungodliness and unrighteousness of men, who suppress the truth in unrighteousness, [19]because that which is known of God is revealed in them, for God revealed it to them. [20]For the invisible things of him since the creation of the world are clearly seen, being perceived through the things that are made, even his everlasting power and divinity; that they may be without excuse. [21]Because, knowing God, they didn't glorify him as God, neither gave thanks, but became vain in their reasoning, and their senseless heart was darkened.

[22]Professing themselves to be wise, they became fools, [23]and traded the glory of the incorruptible God for the likeness of an image of corruptible man, and of birds, and four-footed animals, and creeping things. [24]Therefore God also gave them up in the lusts of their hearts to uncleanness, that their bodies should be dishonored among themselves, [25]who exchanged the truth of God for a lie, and worshiped and served the creature rather than the Creator, who is blessed forever. Amen

[26]For this reason, God gave them up to vile passions. For their women changed the natural function into that which is against nature. [27]Likewise also the men, leaving the natural function of the woman, burned in their lust toward one another, men doing what is inappropriate with men, and receiving in themselves the due penalty of their error. [28]Even as they refused to have God in their knowledge, God gave them up to a reprobate mind, to do those things which are not fitting; [29]being filled with all unrighteousness, sexual immorality, wickedness, covetousness, malice; full of envy, murder, strife, deceit, evil habits, secret slanderers, [30]backbiters, hateful to God, insolent, haughty, boastful, inventors of evil things, disobedient to parents, [31]without understanding, covenant breakers, without natural affection, unforgiving, unmerciful; [32]who, knowing the ordinance of God, that those who practice such things are worthy of death, not only do the same, but also approve of those who practice them.

The apostle Paul explains in this passage that what is known about God is plain. People do not accept the truth about God because they do not want to accept the truth. It is not a lack of information. It is not a lack of reason. What may be known about God is plain. People choose to ignore God and follow their sinful desires because they want to believe in sin.

The most disturbing part of this passage is the revelation that once a person chooses sin over God, God actually gives them over to ever-increasing sin.

Chapter 12

¹He began to speak to them in parables. "A man planted a vineyard, put a hedge around it, dug a pit for the winepress, built a tower, rented it out to a farmer, and went into another country. ²When it was time, he sent a servant to the farmer to get from the farmer his share of the fruit of the vineyard. ³They took him, beat him, and sent him away empty. ⁴Again, he sent another servant to them; and they threw stones at him, wounded him in the head, and sent him away shamefully treated. ⁵Again he sent another; and they killed him; and many others, beating some, and killing some. ⁶Therefore still having one, his beloved son, he sent him last to them, saying, 'They will respect my son.' ⁷But those farmers said among themselves, 'This is the heir. Come, let's kill him, and the inheritance will be ours.' ⁸They took him, killed him, and cast him out of the vineyard. ⁹What therefore will the lord of the vineyard do? He will come and destroy the farmers, and will give the vineyard to others. ¹⁰Haven't you even read this Scripture:

'The stone which the builders rejected,
        the same was made the head of the corner.
¹¹This was from the Lord,
        it is marvelous in our eyes'?"[68]

---

[68]   12:11 Psalm 118:22-23

¹²They tried to seize him, but they feared the multitude; for they perceived that he spoke the parable against them. They left him, and went away.

1. To whom was Jesus speaking?

The religious leaders who confronted him in Mark 11:27, his disciples, and the crowd that was in the Temple courts (Mark 12:12).

2. In this parable, "a man planted a vineyard." Who does that man represent?

God. God created the Jewish religion and the temple worship.

3. Who do the farmers represent?

The Jewish religious leaders. Verse 12 tells us they perceived that the parable was about them.

4. Many servants were sent to the farmers and some were beaten and others were killed. Who do the servants represent?

The prophets that God sent to Israel through the years.

5. The man who planted a vineyard finally sent his son and the farmers killed him. Who is the son in this parable?

Jesus.

6. In verse 9, it says God will give the vineyard "to others." Who are the others?

The Gentiles. This teaches that God will allow his true religion to be open to all people.

7. Do you think the religious leaders talked about Jesus after they left? What do you think they talked about?

They probably said things like, "We cannot let this man continue talking like this. He is stirring up the people to revolt against Rome. Rome allows us to rule the people as long as we keep everyone in line. If we allow this to continue, at the very least, Rome will take our positions of leadership away and appoint Roman governors. At the worst, Rome will crush the rebellion by wiping us off the face of the earth. Jesus must be stopped even if it means killing him."

Mark 12:13-17

[13]They sent some of the Pharisees and of the Herodians to him, that they might trap him with words. [14]When they had come, they asked him, "Teacher, we know that you are honest, and don't defer to anyone; for you aren't partial to anyone, but truly teach the way of God. Is it lawful to pay taxes to Caesar, or not? [15]Shall we give, or shall we not give?"

But he, knowing their hypocrisy, said to them, "Why do you test me? Bring me a denarius, that I may see it."

[16]They brought it.

He said to them, "Whose is this image and inscription?"

They said to him, "Caesar's."

[17]Jesus answered them, "Render to Caesar the things that are Caesar's, and to God the things that are God's."

They marveled greatly at him.

1. **It says someone sent the Pharisees and Herodians. Who might have sent the Pharisees and Herodians?**

The religious leaders from Mark 11:27.

2. **How did they try to trap Jesus?**

The people hated the Romans and hated paying taxes to the Romans. If they could get Jesus to go on record as supporting Rome, they would turn many away from him. If they could get Jesus to go on record as teaching people to defy Rome, they could turn him over to the Romans.

3. What is ironic about this section?

In verse 14, they said Jesus was honest, not swayed by what people thought of him and did not do things to gain popularity, and accurately taught the way of God. This is the exact opposite of the Pharisees and Herodians. If they believed what they said about Jesus, they would have listened to him.

4. How do people today say good things about Jesus but secretly believe something else?

We see politicians and some church leaders make a show of supporting religion but secretly despise morals, justice, and righteousness.

5. Why did he ask about the image on the coin?

The image on the coin was of Caesar. In essence, what Jesus told the crowd was, "give what is created in the image of Caesar to Caesar and give what is created in the image of God to God." We are created in the image of God.

In this statement, Jesus reminds us that what is important is that we are created in the image of God. If a tiny piece of metal created in the image of Caesar has some value, how much more value are we, who are created in the image of God?

Mark 12:18-27

[18]There came to him Sadducees, who say that there is no resurrection. They asked him, saying, [19]"Teacher, Moses wrote to us, 'If a man's brother dies, and leaves a wife behind him, and leaves no children, that his brother should take his wife, and raise up offspring for his brother.' [20]There were seven brothers. The first took a wife, and

dying left no offspring. [21]The second took her, and died, leaving no children behind him. The third likewise; [22]and the seven took her and left no children. Last of all the woman also died. [23]In the resurrection, when they rise, whose wife will she be of them? For the seven had her as a wife."

[24]Jesus answered them, "Isn't this because you are mistaken, not knowing the Scriptures, nor the power of God? [25]For when they will rise from the dead, they neither marry, nor are given in marriage, but are like angels in heaven. [26]But about the dead, that they are raised; haven't you read in the book of Moses, about the Bush, how God spoke to him, saying, 'I am the God of Abraham, the God of Isaac, and the God of Jacob'[69]? [27]He is not the God of the dead, but of the living. You are therefore badly mistaken."

1. Who were the Sadducees, and why was this an absurd question for them?

The Sadducees were another sect or religious group of Jews like the Pharisees. The Sadducees and Pharisees argued with each other, something similar to how the Republicans and Democrats argue today. The Sadducees argued that the written law was the only authority. They rejected the oral tradition of rabbinical teachings that the Pharisees accepted.[1] The Sadducees also rejected the existence of angels and the possibility of a resurrection from the dead and an afterlife.

Acts 23:6-9

[6]But when Paul perceived that the one part were Sadducees and the other Pharisees, he cried out in the council, "Men and brothers, I am a Pharisee, a son of Pharisees. Concerning the hope and resurrection of the dead I am being judged!"

[7]When he had said this, an argument arose between the Pharisees and Sadducees, and the assembly was divided. [8]For the Sadducees

---

[69] [1] Flavius Josephus, *Antiquities of the Jews*, 13.10.6

[12:26] Exodus 3:6

say that there is no resurrection, nor angel, nor spirit; but the Pharisees confess all of these. ⁹A great clamor arose, and some of the scribes of the Pharisees part stood up, and contended, saying, "We find no evil in this man. But if a spirit or angel has spoken to him, let's not fight against God!"

In Mark 12, the Sadducees attempted to trap Jesus by asking a question about the resurrection. This question was a hypothetical question that the Sadducees used against the Pharisees to win debates. They postulated that if there was a resurrection from the dead, as the Pharisees claimed, absurd situations would ensue.

Jesus corrected them by saying that people who are resurrected from the dead will be unmarried, like the angels (which the Sadducees did not believe in). That is great irony. Then Jesus quoted from Exodus 3:6 (one of the first five books of the Old Testament, also known as The Torah).

Exodus 3:6 speaks in the present tense, not the past tense. God identified himself to Moses saying, "I am the God of Abraham, the God of Isaac and the God of Jacob." Jesus is arguing that if God meant to say, "I am the God who was God to Abraham" (implying Abraham is dead and gone), God would have used the past tense and said, "I was the God of Abraham." Using past tense would mean, When Abraham was alive, I was his God."

But Moses recorded that God said, "I am the God of Abraham." The present tense implies that Abraham, Isaac, and Jacob are alive.

Is God the God of dead people or living people? In verse 27, Jesus declared that God is the God of the living. Now, the Sadducees are on the horns of a dilemma. If they try to argue that Exodus 3:6 is in the present tense but should be interpreted in past tense, then they claim God is the God of the dead—which is the inescapable conclusion of their belief that there is no afterlife. God is the God of the living because the resurrection is true.

2. How do you think the afterlife is different than the life here?

It seems that some of the Christians in Corinth were also influenced by the teachings of the Sadducees. It is possible that some Sadducees had become Christians and were holding to their life-long beliefs, still rejecting resurrection and life after death. Whatever the circumstance in Corinth, Paul addresses the teaching at length in 1 Corinthians 15.

1 Corinthians 15:12-58

[12]Now if Christ is preached, that he has been raised from the dead, how do some among you say that there is no resurrection of the dead? [13]But if there is no resurrection of the dead, neither has Christ been raised. [14]If Christ has not been raised, then our preaching is in vain, and your faith also is in vain. [15]Yes, we are found false witnesses of God, because we testified about God that he raised up Christ, whom he didn't raise up, if it is so that the dead are not raised. [16]For if the dead aren't raised, neither has Christ been raised. [17]If Christ has not been raised, your faith is vain; you are still in your sins. [18]Then they also who are fallen asleep in Christ have perished. [19]If we have only hoped in Christ in this life, we are of all men most pitiable.

[20]But now Christ has been raised from the dead. He became the first fruits of those who are asleep. [21]For since death came by man, the resurrection of the dead also came by man. [22]For as in Adam all die, so also in Christ all will be made alive. [23]But each in his own order: Christ the first fruits, then those who are Christ's, at his coming. [24]Then the end comes, when he will deliver up the kingdom to God, even the Father; when he will have abolished all rule and all authority and power. [25]For he must reign until he has put all his enemies under his feet. [26]The last enemy that will be abolished is death. [27]For, "He put all things in subjection under his feet."[70] But when he says, "All things are put in subjection," it is evident that he is excepted who subjected all things to him. [28]When all things have been subjected to him, then the Son will also himself be subjected to him who subjected all things to him, that God may be all in all. [29]Or else what will they do who are baptized for the dead? If the

---

[70]   15:27 Psalm 8:6

dead aren't raised at all, why then are they baptized for the dead? [30]Why do we also stand in jeopardy every hour? [31]I affirm, by the boasting in you which I have in Christ Jesus our Lord, I die daily. [32]If I fought with animals at Ephesus for human purposes, what does it profit me? If the dead are not raised, then "let us eat and drink, for tomorrow we die."[71] [33]Don't be deceived! "Evil companionships corrupt good morals." [34]Wake up righteously, and don't sin, for some have no knowledge of God. I say this to your shame. [35]But someone will say, "How are the dead raised?" and, "With what kind of body do they come?" [36]You foolish one, that which you yourself sow is not made alive unless it dies. [37]That which you sow, you don't sow the body that will be, but a bare grain, maybe of wheat, or of some other kind. [38]But God gives it a body even as it pleased him, and to each seed a body of its own. [39]All flesh is not the same flesh, but there is one flesh of men, another flesh of animals, another of fish, and another of birds. [40]There are also celestial bodies, and terrestrial bodies; but the glory of the celestial differs from that of the terrestrial. [41]There is one glory of the sun, another glory of the moon, and another glory of the stars; for one star differs from another star in glory. [42]So also is the resurrection of the dead. It is sown in corruption; it is raised in incorruption. [43]It is sown in dishonor; it is raised in glory. It is sown in weakness; it is raised in power. [44]It is sown a natural body; it is raised a spiritual body. There is a natural body and there is also a spiritual body.

[45]So also it is written, "The first man, Adam, became a living soul."[72] The last Adam became a life-giving spirit. [46]However that which is spiritual isn't first, but that which is natural, then that which is spiritual. [47]The first man is of the earth, made of dust. The second man is the Lord from heaven. [48]As is the one made of dust, such are those who are also made of dust; and as is the heavenly, such are they also that are heavenly. [49]As we have borne the image of those made of dust, let's[73] also bear the image of the heavenly. [50]Now I

---

[71]   15:32 Isaiah 22:13

[72]   15:45 Genesis 2:7

[73]   15:49 NU, TR read "we will" instead of "let's."

say this, brothers,[74] that flesh and blood can't inherit the kingdom of God; neither does corruption inherit incorruption.

[51]Behold, I tell you a mystery. We will not all sleep, but we will all be changed, [52]in a moment, in the twinkling of an eye, at the last trumpet. For the trumpet will sound, and the dead will be raised incorruptible, and we will be changed. [53]For this corruptible must put on incorruption, and this mortal must put on immortality. [54]But when this corruptible will have put on incorruption, and this mortal will have put on immortality, then what is written will happen:

"Death is swallowed up in victory."[75]

[55]"Death, where is your sting?

Hades[76], where is your victory?"[77]

[56]The sting of death is sin, and the power of sin is the law. [57]But thanks be to God, who gives us the victory through our Lord Jesus Christ. [58]Therefore, my beloved brothers, be steadfast, immovable, always abounding in the Lord's work, because you know that your labor is not in vain in the Lord.

The apostle Paul describes the resurrection of Jesus Christ as the central and essential proof of Christianity. All of Christianity stands or falls on this one point. If Jesus was raised from the dead, then there is a resurrection and life after death. If Jesus was not raised from the dead, then Christians have no hope and should be pitied above all others.

---

[74] 15:50 The word for "brothers" here and where context allows may also be correctly translated "brothers and sisters" or "siblings."

[75] 15:54 Isaiah 25:8

[76] 15:55 or, Hell

[77] 15:55 Hosea 13:14

Mark 12:28–34

[28]One of the scribes came, and heard them questioning together. Knowing that he had answered them well, asked him, "Which commandment is the greatest of all?"

[29]Jesus answered, "The greatest is, 'Hear, Israel, the Lord our God, the Lord is one: [30]you shall love the Lord your God with all your heart, and with all your soul, and with all your mind, and with all your strength.'[78] This is the first commandment. [31]The second is like this, 'You shall love your neighbor as yourself.'[79] There is no other commandment greater than these."

[32]The scribe said to him, "Truly, teacher, you have said well that he is one, and there is none other but he, [33]and to love him with all the heart, and with all the understanding, with all the soul, and with all the strength, and to love his neighbor as himself, is more important than all whole burnt offerings and sacrifices."

[34]When Jesus saw that he answered wisely, he said to him, "You are not far from the kingdom of God."

No one dared ask him any question after that.

1.   Who asked Jesus a question, and how was this different than the other religious leaders?

A scribe or teacher of the law asked this final question. In verse 28, it says that the scribe heard Jesus answering well. This probably indicates that the questioned posed was asked with respect instead of jealousy.

The question solicited a recitation of the Shema, the core of the Jewish religion. Even today, the Shema is recited at the beginning of every synagogue service. Jesus added Leviticus 19:18, which was amazingly insightful given where they were. They were at the Temple where people

---

[78]   12:30 Deuteronomy 6:4–5
[79]   12:31 Leviticus 19:18

were offering sacrifices to atone for their sins. All sin is either against God or against other people. If people loved God with all their hearts, soul, mind, and strength, and loved their neighbors as themselves, there would be no need for animal sacrifices. The scribe grasped the importance of what Jesus said, if not the whole meaning. Jesus told him he was close to the kingdom of God.

2. Why was the scribe close to the kingdom of God rather than in it?

The kingdom of God, in the sense of fulfilling prophecy, would not be established until Jesus sat at the right hand of God and began to rule. This happened at the Ascension.

Mark 12:35-37

> [35]Jesus responded, as he taught in the temple, "How is it that the scribes say that the Christ is the son of David? [36]For David himself said in the Holy Spirit,
>
> > 'The Lord said to my Lord,
> > > "Sit at my right hand,
> > > until I make your enemies the footstool of your
> > feet."'[80]
>
> [37]Therefore David himself calls him Lord, so how can he be his son?"
>
> The common people heard him gladly.

1. Why did Mark choose to follow the discussion about the kingdom of God with this question?

Jesus quoted Psalm 110:1, which is one of the prophecies about the Christ, or Messiah, sitting at the right hand of the Lord. It is kingdom

---

[80]   12:36 Psalm 110:1

language. It is a natural segue from talking about the kingdom of God to a question about Psalm 110.

2. What did Jesus really ask?

The scribes correctly taught that the Christ would come from the lineage (or be a descendant) of David. Matthew 1:6 and Luke 3:31 clearly show that Jesus did come from the lineage of—David—at least from his human ancestry. Remember, the point of the book of Mark is about the true identity of Jesus. Jesus was revealing the true meaning of Psalm 110.

David wrote Psalm 110 and started it by saying, "The Lord (meaning God) said to my Lord (meaning the Christ or Messiah) sit at my right hand . . ." David never sat at the right hand of God. The Messiah is not just "Son of David" (which Jesus was called in Mark 10:47-48, Matthew 9:27; 12:23). Jesus is "Son of God."

Mark 12:38-44

[38]In his teaching he said to them, "Beware of the scribes, who like to walk in long robes, and to get greetings in the marketplaces, [39]and the best seats in the synagogues, and the best places at feasts: [40]those who devour widows' houses, and for a pretense make long prayers. These will receive greater condemnation."

[41]Jesus sat down opposite the treasury, and saw how the multitude cast money into the treasury. Many who were rich cast in much. [42]A poor widow came, and she cast in two small brass coins,[81] which equal a quadrans coin.[82] [43]He called his disciples to himself, and said to them, "Most certainly I tell you, this poor widow gave more than all those who are giving into the treasury, [44]for they all

---

[81] 12:42 literally, lepta (or widow's mites). Lepta are very small brass coins worth half a quadrans each, which is a quarter of the copper assarion. Lepta are worth less than 1% of an agricultural worker's daily wages.

[82] 12:42 A quadrans is a coin worth about 1/64 of a denarius. A denarius is about one day's wages for an agricultural laborer.

gave out of their abundance, but she, out of her poverty, gave all that she had to live on."

(Note: Jesus continued the discussion about the Jewish leaders and mentioned how they devour widows' houses. He then shows how the poor widow gave more than the religious leaders.)

1. The theme in this chapter is the confrontation with the religious leaders. How does this section fit with the theme, and is it a fitting conclusion?

The religious leaders confronted Jesus and tried to trap him with their questions. He answered with deep spiritual truths and uncovered the hypocrisy of these religious leaders. This final description of the hypocrites includes the charge that they devour the estates of widows. In other words, they feed on the needy.

2. How does the teaching about giving fit this context?

Jesus taught that the religious leaders devour the estates of widows. He then turns around and shows how this widow was more righteous than the hypocritical religious leaders.

Chapter 13

Mark 13:1-4

¹As he went out of the temple, one of his disciples said to him, "Teacher, see what kind of stones and what kind of buildings!"

²Jesus said to him, "Do you see these great buildings? There will not be left here one stone on another, which will not be thrown down."

³As he sat on the Mount of Olives opposite the temple, Peter, James, John, and Andrew asked him privately, ⁴"Tell us, when will these things be? What is the sign that these things are all about to be fulfilled?"

(Note: Because Matthew 24 contains more detail than Mark 13, it is helpful to use Matthew for a fuller understanding of what Jesus is teaching.)

Matthew 24:1-3

¹Jesus went out from the temple, and was going on his way. His disciples came to him to show him the buildings of the temple. ²But he answered them, "You see all of these things, don't you? Most certainly I tell you, there will not be left here one stone on another, that will not be thrown down."

³As he sat on the Mount of Olives, the disciples came to him privately, saying, "Tell us, when will these things be? What is the sign of your coming, and of the end of the age?"

1. The disciples marveled at the construction and architecture of the Jewish Temple. What did Jesus predict?

He predicted the destruction of the Temple. This was not the first time. He predicted the siege and destruction of the Temple in Luke 19:36–46 during his triumphal entry. Historically, the actual destruction of the Temple occurred in 70 A.D. after a three-year siege on the city.

2. When they were on the Mount of Olives, possibly in view of the Temple in distance, the disciples asked some questions in private. Why in private?

Talking about the destruction of the Temple was heresy. Temple worship and animal sacrifices were at the core of Judaism at this time. They believed their God lived in that temple. It was bad enough that the land promised to Abraham and his descendants had been taken over by the Romans. The Temple was still under Jewish control and run by the priests. It was unthinkable to the Jews that God, who lived in the Temple, would allow it to be taken by Romans.

3. How many questions did the disciples ask and exactly what were they asking?

Matthew records these three questions while Mark used more general language to lump the questions into two. To the disciples, it did not matter if they were asking two or three questions because it was all the same question, "When do we start the revolution?"

The question was motivated by their desire to engage the Romans in war. In Mark 6, they had gathered the beginning of an army, and it seemed to be in response to the murder of John the Baptist. In John 6:15, the 5,000 were ready to make Jesus king by force. If the murder of their prophet, John the Baptist, was not the beginning trigger of the revolution, what would be? The Romans attacking the Temple, the very heart of Judaism, would certainly be enough trigger for an all out war.

When they asked, "When will these things be?" They were asking Jesus, "When will the Temple be destroyed like you said?" When they asked, "What is the sign of your coming?" they were asking,

"What sign can we look for that will signal your coming into power as king over the whole earth?" When they asked, "What is the sign of the end of the age?" they were asking about the end of the age of Jewish punishment for disobedience to God that had been continuing for 483 years, as prophesied in Daniel and included domination by the Babylonians, Assyrians, Greeks, and Romans. The Messianic prophecies described the return of glory and favor with the coming of the King, the Messiah. The Messiah was going to be king over the whole earth. They thought that meant taking the place of Caesar. In their world, Caesar was king over the whole known world. This would usher in a new age where Israel and the Jews were the rightful rulers. The Gentiles were dogs that would pay tribute to them instead of the Jews paying tribute to Rome. It would be a new age.

These were the questions the disciples asked. Jesus gave answers that they did not expect.

Matthew 24:4-14

> [4]Jesus answered them, "Be careful that no one leads you astray. [5]For many will come in my name, saying, 'I am the Christ,' and will lead many astray. [6]You will hear of wars and rumors of wars. See that you aren't troubled, for all this must happen, but the end is not yet. [7]For nation will rise against nation, and kingdom against kingdom; and there will be famines, plagues, and earthquakes in various places. [8]But all these things are the beginning of birth pains. [9]Then they will deliver you up to oppression, and will kill you. You will be hated by all of the nations for my name's sake. [10]Then many will stumble, and will deliver up one another, and will hate one another. [11]Many false prophets will arise, and will lead many astray. [12]Because iniquity will be multiplied, the love of many will grow cold. [13]But he who endures to the end, the same will be saved. [14]This Good News of the kingdom will be preached in the whole world for a testimony to all the nations, and then the end will come.

1. What question is Jesus answering?

This answer fits the first question, "When will these things be?" Jesus said, "You see these stones of the Temple? Not one will be left on another." So, the disciples asked him, "When will these things be? When will the Temple be destroyed?"

2. Does the language sound like events leading up to the destruction of the Temple or events leading to the end of the world and Jesus' Second Coming?

The literary and historical contexts demand that Jesus' answer be referring to the destruction of the Temple. Each of these predictions were easily fulfilled in events that occurred between 30 A.D. and 70 A.D. It is documented that many Zealots and Jews claimed to be Messiah during this time and tried to start revolutions against Rome. There were wars and rumors of war in this time. There were earthquakes in various places, including at the time of Jesus' death. The book of Acts documents how the disciples were beaten in synagogues and stood before kings to testify about Jesus. Colossians 1:23 records that the Gospel was preached to all creation, fulfilling the prediction that the Good News be preached to all nations. Disciples were even betrayed by their own families and persecuted and martyred. All the things Jesus predicted and warned about came true in the decades after the resurrection and before 70 A.D.

Matthew 24:4-14 can easily be attributed as describing events leading up to the destruction of the Temple.

3. Verse 12 states that wickedness will increase and the love of many will grow cold. Is there a correlation between wickedness and love?

As discussed earlier, the greatest commandments, to love God with all your heart, soul, mind, and strength, and to love your neighbor as yourself, are the true path to righteousness. If you love God, you will not worship other gods nor take his name in vane. If you love people, you will not rob them, lie to them, cheat them, etc. For wickedness to increase, there must be a corresponding reduction in love. As love grows cold and people become more selfish, wickedness will surely increase.

Matthew 24:15-25

[15]"When, therefore, you see the abomination of desolation,[83] which was spoken of through Daniel the prophet, standing in the holy place (let the reader understand), [16]then let those who are in Judea flee to the mountains. [17]Let him who is on the housetop not go down to take out things that are in his house. [18]Let him who is in the field not return back to get his clothes. [19]But woe to those who are with child and to nursing mothers in those days! [20]Pray that your flight will not be in the winter, nor on a Sabbath, [21]for then there will be great oppression, such as has not been from the beginning of the world until now, no, nor ever will be. [22]Unless those days had been shortened, no flesh would have been saved. But for the sake of the chosen ones, those days will be shortened.

[23]"Then if any man tells you, 'Behold, here is the Christ,' or, 'There,' don't believe it. [24]For there will arise false christs, and false prophets, and they will show great signs and wonders, so as to lead astray, if possible, even the chosen ones. [25]"Behold, I have told you beforehand.

(Note: The Old Testament book Daniel contains prophecies that specifically defined when the Messiah would appear. It also foretold the destruction of the Temple by the Romans and used the phrase, "the abomination that causes desolation.")

1. Is there anything in Matthew 24:15-25 that might not be describing events leading up to the destruction of the Temple in 70 A.D.?

No, the disciples would have understood that Jesus was telling them what would happen at the time of the destruction of the Temple.

---

[83]   24:15 Daniel 9:27; 11:31; 12:11

Matthew 24:26-35

[26]If therefore they tell you, 'Behold, he is in the wilderness,' don't go out; 'Behold, he is in the inner rooms,' don't believe it. [27]For as the lightning flashes from the east, and is seen even to the west, so will be the coming of the Son of Man. [28]For wherever the carcass is, there is where the vultures[84] gather together. [29]But immediately after the oppression of those days, the sun will be darkened, the moon will not give its light, the stars will fall from the sky, and the powers of the heavens will be shaken;[85] [30]and then the sign of the Son of Man will appear in the sky. Then all the tribes of the earth will mourn, and they will see the Son of Man coming on the clouds of the sky with power and great glory. [31]He will send out his angels with a great sound of a trumpet, and they will gather together his chosen ones from the four winds, from one end of the sky to the other.

[32]"Now from the fig tree learn this parable. When its branch has now become tender, and puts forth its leaves, you know that the summer is near. [33]Even so you also, when you see all these things, know that it is near, even at the doors. [34]Most certainly I tell you, this generation[86] will not pass away, until all these things are accomplished. [35]Heaven and earth will pass away, but my words will not pass away.

1. **Does this language sound like the destruction of the Temple in 70 A.D. or the Second Coming?**

This language sounds like the Second Coming of Christ.

2. **How did we go from talking about the destruction of the Temple in 70 A.D. to the Second Coming and the end of the world (age)?**

---

[84]   24:28 or, eagles
[85]   24:29 Isaiah 13:10; 34:4
[86]   24:34 The word for "generation" (genea) can also be translated as "race."

In Mark 10, James and John asked to be at Jesus' right and left hands. Jesus replied in Mark 10:38, "You do not know what you are asking."

In Matthew 24, when the disciples asked, "When will these things be? What is the sign of your coming and of the end of the age?" they did not know what they were asking. They thought they were asking one question, "When do we start the war and make you king by force?" Jesus took the opportunity to tell them about the destruction of the Temple but also about his coming at the end of the age. It was a very different answer than they expected.

3. Describe how "The Son of Man" will come.

There will be signs in the sun, moon, and stars, and all nations will see the Son of Man coming in the clouds with power and glory, and the angels will gather the elect from the four winds.

4. Verse 29 says, "Immediately after the oppression of those days . . ." Surely the oppression discussed is the destruction of Jerusalem in 70 A.D. (see verse 21). Jesus said, "immediately after." Did his Second Coming happen immediately after 70 A.D.? How do you explain this?

One answer is that the oppression against the Jews in 70 A.D. has continued to this day and has not yet ended. The fact that the Temple has never been rebuilt and persecution of the Jews continues is evidence that the oppression continues. When it ends, we can reach a time "immediately after the oppression."

Another answer is that Jesus did come immediately after the destruction of Jerusalem and his coming was his inauguration as the King of Kings and Lord of Lords when he sat down at the right hand of God. The figurative language, such as angels, the sun, moon, and stars, was meant to convey how grand and powerful the event was in a spiritual realm.

Matthew 24:36–51

[36]But no one knows of that day and hour, not even the angels of heaven,[87] but my Father only.

[37]"As the days of Noah were, so will be the coming of the Son of Man. [38]For as in those days which were before the flood they were eating and drinking, marrying and giving in marriage, until the day that Noah entered into the ship, [39]and they didn't know until the flood came, and took them all away, so will be the coming of the Son of Man. [40]Then two men will be in the field: one will be taken and one will be left; [41]two women grinding at the mill, one will be taken and one will be left. [42]Watch therefore, for you don't know in what hour your Lord comes. [43]But know this, that if the master of the house had known in what watch of the night the thief was coming, he would have watched, and would not have allowed his house to be broken into. [44]Therefore also be ready, for in an hour that you don't expect, the Son of Man will come.

[45]"Who then is the faithful and wise servant, whom his lord has set over his household, to give them their food in due season? [46]Blessed is that servant whom his lord finds doing so when he comes. [47]Most certainly I tell you that he will set him over all that he has. [48]But if that evil servant should say in his heart, 'My lord is delaying his coming,' [49]and begins to beat his fellow servants, and eat and drink with the drunkards, [50]the lord of that servant will come in a day when he doesn't expect it, and in an hour when he doesn't know it, [51]and will cut him in pieces, and appoint his portion with the hypocrites. There is where the weeping and grinding of teeth will be.

1. **If no one knows the day Jesus will return, why should we believe people who predict the Second Coming will be on a specific day?**

---

[87] 24:36 NU adds "nor the son"

When preachers and prophets publicize a specific date for the return of Jesus and the end of the world, they do it in opposition to verse 36. Jesus can return at any time.

2. What is Jesus saying when he likens the Second Coming to the time of Noah? What point is Jesus making?

The people in Noah's day were eating and drinking and marrying and carrying on with life while ignoring Noah's warnings. One day, Noah got into his ship and closed the doors, and the people, so preoccupied with the duties of daily life, died. Jesus' point is that another day is coming, and we better be more attentive to spiritual things than the people of Noah's day were. We need to watch and pay attention.

3. Verses 31, 40, and 41 have been woven together to create the concept of a "rapture." The rapture is a time when all believers are supposed to leave the planet at the same time and non-believers are left behind. Do these verses teach that?

The interesting concept in using verses 40 and 41 to prove a rapture is that, today, we think being taken is a good thing. In their culture, foreign armies came through and took people to serve as slaves. To first-century Jews, being taken was a very bad thing. The first-century audience hearing this prediction would want to be the ones left. They would interpret the phrase, "some would be taken" to mean the opposite of what modern readers often conclude. They would not have understood this as speaking of the rapture.

4. What is the difference between a person who is expecting his master's return and one who is not?

The one who expects an eminent return stays prepared and remains faithful.

5. If Jesus could return at any time, how do you prepare?

Become a disciple of Jesus, a Christian, and get in a good, Bible-believing church. Do not be caught involved in sin. Be faithful.

Chapter 14

[1]It was now two days before the feast of the Passover and the unleavened bread, and the chief priests and the scribes sought how they might seize him by deception, and kill him. [2]For they said, "Not during the feast, because there might be a riot of the people."

[3]While he was at Bethany, in the house of Simon the leper, as he sat at the table, a woman came having an alabaster jar of ointment of pure nard—very costly. She broke the jar, and poured it over his head. [4]But there were some who were indignant among themselves, saying, "Why has this ointment been wasted? [5]For this might have been sold for more than three hundred denarii,[88] and given to the poor." They grumbled against her.

[6]But Jesus said, "Leave her alone. Why do you trouble her? She has done a good work for me. [7]For you always have the poor with you, and whenever you want to, you can do them good; but you will not always have me. [8]She has done what she could. She has anointed my body beforehand for the burying. [9]Most certainly I tell you, wherever this Good News may be preached throughout the whole world, that which this woman has done will also be spoken of for a memorial of her."

---

[88]   14:5 300 denarii was about a years wages for an agricultural laborer.

[10]Judas Iscariot, who was one of the twelve, went away to the chief priests, that he might deliver him to them. [11]They, when they heard it, were glad, and promised to give him money. He sought how he might conveniently deliver him.

1. **Following chiastic patterns, Mark put the story of the woman anointing Jesus between the discussion of the chief priests in verses 1-2 and 10-11. Why is this an important event? Was this Jesus' anointing as king?**

In 1 Samuel 16:13, the prophet Samuel, following God's instructions, anointed David as king over Israel. Anointing, in these cases, was the same as coronation. In Acts 10:34-38, Peter explained that God anointed Jesus with the Holy Spirit and power at Jesus' baptism. Jesus was anointed by God. What this woman did, as explained by Jesus, was to prepare his body for burial. It was presented in contrast to what the corrupt religious leaders of Jesus' day were doing to him.

2. **Does it seem out of character that the religious leaders wanted to seize Jesus by deception and kill him?**

Yes, it is ironic that men who try to appear righteous and pious would be plotting deception and murder. John gives more detail in John 11:45-57.

John 11:45-57

[45]Therefore many of the Jews, who came to Mary and saw what Jesus did, believed in him. [46]But some of them went away to the Pharisees, and told them the things which Jesus had done. [47]The chief priests therefore and the Pharisees gathered a council, and said, "What are we doing? For this man does many signs. [48]If we leave him alone like this, everyone will believe in him, and the Romans will come and take away both our place and our nation."

[49]But a certain one of them, Caiaphas, being high priest that year, said to them, "You know nothing at all, [50]nor do you consider that it is advantageous for us that one man should die for the people, and that the whole nation not perish." [51]Now he didn't say this of

himself, but being high priest that year, he prophesied that Jesus would die for the nation, [52]and not for the nation only, but that he might also gather together into one the children of God who are scattered abroad. [53]So from that day forward they took counsel that they might put him to death. [54]Jesus therefore walked no more openly among the Jews, but departed from there into the country near the wilderness, to a city called Ephraim. He stayed there with his disciples.

[55]Now the Passover of the Jews was at hand. Many went up from the country to Jerusalem before the Passover, to purify themselves. [56]Then they sought for Jesus and spoke one with another, as they stood in the temple, "What do you think—that he isn't coming to the feast at all?" [57]Now the chief priests and the Pharisees had commanded that if anyone knew where he was, he should report it, that they might seize him.

It is interesting to see how corrupt religious leaders can justify murder. Christianity is today's true religion and must never tolerate people who claim to be religious but plot deception and murder.

3. **Mark states that two days before the Passover and Feast of Unleavened Bread, the chief priests and scribes were looking for a way to arrest Jesus. John states that Jesus arrived in Bethany six days before Passover. Mark says a woman poured perfume on Jesus' head, and John says Mary poured perfume on his feet. How do you reconcile the details of these descriptions?**

Nothing here is contradictory. Jesus could have certainly arrived in Bethany six days before the Passover, and the meal honoring Jesus could have been two days before the Feast. The woman could certainly have been named Mary, and she could have anointed his head and feet. All statements could be true. It just depends on which details a particular writer wanted to include.

4. **Mark 14:3 says that Jesus came to Bethany and was at the house of Simon the Leper. Is it strange that Jesus would be at a leper's house?**

John tells us that this house in Bethany was the home of Mary, Martha, and Lazarus. This is the same Lazarus that Jesus raised from the dead in John 11. This means that either Simon the Leper was a fourth member of the household or, as some speculate, Lazarus was also called Simon and was a leper. Obviously, Jesus had no issues with staying at a leper's home. It is probable that Jesus healed him.

John 12:1-11

[1]Then six days before the Passover, Jesus came to Bethany, where Lazarus was, who had been dead, whom he raised from the dead. [2]So they made him a supper there. Martha served, but Lazarus was one of those who sat at the table with him. [3]Mary, therefore, took a pound[89] of ointment of pure nard, very precious, and anointed the feet of Jesus, and wiped his feet with her hair. The house was filled with the fragrance of the ointment. [4]Then Judas Iscariot, Simon's son, one of his disciples, who would betray him, said, [5]"Why wasn't this ointment sold for three hundred denarii,[90] and given to the poor?" [6]Now he said this, not because he cared for the poor, but because he was a thief, and having the money box, used to steal what was put into it. [7]But Jesus said, "Leave her alone. She has kept this for the day of my burial. [8]For you always have the poor with you, but you don't always have me."

[9]A large crowd therefore of the Jews learned that he was there, and they came, not for Jesus' sake only, but that they might see Lazarus also, whom he had raised from the dead. [10]But the chief priests conspired to put Lazarus to death also, [11]because on account of him many of the Jews went away and believed in Jesus.

5. **After the discussion about the woman, in Mark 14:10-11, Judas goes out to betray Jesus. Why did Judas conspire to betray Jesus?**

---

[89] 12:3 a Roman pound of 12 ounces, or about 340 grams.
[90] 12:5 300 denarii was about a year's wages for an agricultural laborer.

Some speculate that Judas wanted money. John clearly states that Judas was a thief (John 12:6) and stole money from the communal money box. Seeing this very valuable perfumed ointment used on Jesus instead of receiving the money may have been too much for Judas.

Others suggest that, while Judas was a greedy thief, he may have also been a patriot wanting to fight the Romans and free the Jews. Judas might have believed that getting Jesus arrested was the best way to start a revolution. His followers would have to fight to free Jesus and that would trigger the revolution.

When Judas realized his actions led to Jesus being crucified, he gave the blood money back and committed suicide (Matthew 27:3). This does not sound like a thief who acted for purely selfish gain.

Mark 14:12-26

12On the first day of unleavened bread, when they sacrificed the Passover, his disciples asked him, "Where do you want us to go and prepare that you may eat the Passover?"

13He sent two of his disciples, and said to them, "Go into the city, and there you will meet a man carrying a pitcher of water. Follow him, 14and wherever he enters in, tell the master of the house, 'The Teacher says, "Where is the guest room, where I may eat the Passover with my disciples?"' 15He will himself show you a large upper room furnished and ready. Get ready for us there."

16His disciples went out, and came into the city, and found things as he had said to them, and they prepared the Passover.

17When it was evening he came with the twelve. 18As they sat and were eating, Jesus said, "Most certainly I tell you, one of you will betray me—he who eats with me."

19They began to be sorrowful, and to ask him one by one, "Surely not I?" And another said, "Surely not I?"

[20]He answered them, "It is one of the twelve, he who dips with me in the dish. [21]For the Son of Man goes, even as it is written about him, but woe to that man by whom the Son of Man is betrayed! It would be better for that man if he had not been born."

[22]As they were eating, Jesus took bread, and when he had blessed, he broke it, and gave to them, and said, "Take, eat. This is my body."

[23]He took the cup, and when he had given thanks, he gave to them. They all drank of it. [24]He said to them, "This is my blood of the new covenant, which is poured out for many. [25]Most certainly I tell you, I will no more drink of the fruit of the vine, until that day when I drink it anew in the kingdom of God." [26]When they had sung a hymn, they went out to the Mount of Olives.

1. **How did Jesus know a man would be carrying a pitcher of water and, therefore, lead the disciples to the place prepared for the special dinner?**

It was Jewish custom to offer hospitality (or rent available rooms) to pilgrims visiting Jerusalem for the Feast. A man carrying a pitcher of water would be preparing such a room. It is probable that Jesus was telling the two disciples (identified as Peter and John in Luke 22:8) to go find one of the rooms being prepared and secure its use.

2. **Jesus knew what Judas was about to do and prophesied the betrayal before it happened. Did Judas have a free-will choice to betray Jesus or not betray him? Because it was destined to happen, did Judas still have a choice?**

The question is whether influence was exerted on Judas. Just knowing how someone would choose does not necessarily influence the choice. Philosophers argue that without choice, there is no responsibility. In other words, if God forced Judas to betray Jesus and there was no other option for Judas, then how could God hold Judas responsible for the betrayal? On the other hand, if Judas was planning the betrayal and Jesus could tell what choice was going to be made, Judas still had a free-will choice and was responsible because no influence or force made Judas do what he did.

3. **Matthew, Mark, Luke, and John give four different accounts of the evening and emphasize different things. How do you harmonize the accounts?**

Matthew 26:20-29

[20]Now when evening had come, he was reclining at the table with the twelve disciples. [21]As they were eating, he said, "Most certainly I tell you that one of you will betray me."

[22]They were exceedingly sorrowful, and each began to ask him, "It isn't me, is it, Lord?"

[23]He answered, "He who dipped his hand with me in the dish, the same will betray me. [24]The Son of Man goes, even as it is written of him, but woe to that man through whom the Son of Man is betrayed! It would be better for that man if he had not been born."

[25]Judas, who betrayed him, answered, "It isn't me, is it, Rabbi?"

He said to him, "You said it."

[26]As they were eating, Jesus took bread, gave thanks for[91] it, and broke it. He gave to the disciples, and said, "Take, eat; this is my body." [27]He took the cup, gave thanks, and gave to them, saying, "All of you drink it, [28]for this is my blood of the new covenant, which is poured out for many for the remission of sins. [29]But I tell you that I will not drink of this fruit of the vine from now on, until that day when I drink it anew with you in my Father's kingdom."

---

[91] 26:26 TR reads "blessed" instead of "gave thanks for"

Luke 22:14-30

[14]When the hour had come, he sat down with the twelve apostles. [15]He said to them, "I have earnestly desired to eat this Passover with you before I suffer, [16]for I tell you, I will no longer by any means eat of it until it is fulfilled in the kingdom of God." [17]He received a cup, and when he had given thanks, he said, "Take this, and share it among yourselves, [18]for I tell you, I will not drink at all again from the fruit of the vine, until the kingdom of God comes."

[19]He took bread, and when he had given thanks, he broke it, and gave to them, saying, "This is my body which is given for you. Do this in memory of me." [20]Likewise, he took the cup after supper, saying, "This cup is the new covenant in my blood, which is poured out for you. [21]But behold, the hand of him who betrays me is with me on the table. [22]The Son of Man indeed goes, as it has been determined, but woe to that man through whom he is betrayed!"

[23]They began to question among themselves, which of them it was who would do this thing. [24]There arose also a contention among them, which of them was considered to be greatest. [25]He said to them, "The kings of the nations lord it over them, and those who have authority over them are called 'benefactors.' [26]But not so with you. But one who is the greater among you, let him become as the younger, and one who is governing, as one who serves. [27]For who is greater, one who sits at the table, or one who serves? Isn't it he who sits at the table? But I am in the midst of you as one who serves. [28]But you are those who have continued with me in my trials. [29]I confer on you a kingdom, even as my Father conferred on me, [30]that you may eat and drink at my table in my kingdom. You will sit on thrones, judging the twelve tribes of Israel."

John 13:18-30

[18]I don't speak concerning all of you. I know whom I have chosen. But that the Scripture may be fulfilled, 'He who eats bread with

me has lifted up his heel against me.'[92] [19]From now on, I tell you before it happens, that when it happens, you may believe that I am he. [20]Most certainly I tell you, he who receives whomever I send, receives me; and he who receives me, receives him who sent me."

[21]When Jesus had said this, he was troubled in spirit, and testified, "Most certainly I tell you that one of you will betray me."

[22]The disciples looked at one another, perplexed about whom he spoke. [23]One of his disciples, whom Jesus loved, was at the table, leaning against Jesus' breast. [24]Simon Peter therefore beckoned to him, and said to him, "Tell us who it is of whom he speaks."

[25]He, leaning back, as he was, on Jesus' breast, asked him, "Lord, who is it?"

[26]Jesus therefore answered, "It is he to whom I will give this piece of bread when I have dipped it." So when he had dipped the piece of bread, he gave it to Judas, the son of Simon Iscariot. [27]After the piece of bread, then Satan entered into him.

Then Jesus said to him, "What you do, do quickly."

[28]Now no man at the table knew why he said this to him. [29]For some thought, because Judas had the money box, that Jesus said to him, "Buy what things we need for the feast," or that he should give something to the poor. [30]Therefore having received that morsel, he went out immediately. It was night.

The accounts of Matthew and Mark begin with Jesus foretelling the betrayal. They follow with the institution of Communion and mention the kingdom of God.

Luke begins with the sharing of a cup and a longer message about the kingdom of God. Luke emphasizes the kingdom of God and the

---

[92]   13:18 Psalm 41:9

fact that Jesus will not taste the fruit of the vine until they all take Communion in the kingdom.

In Matthew, Mark, and Luke, Jesus took bread, gave thanks, broke it, and gave it to the disciples. In Matthew and Mark, Jesus explained what he was doing with the bread saying, "Take, eat, this is my body." Luke gives the extended version, "This is my body which is given for you. Do this in memory of me." In Luke's account, Jesus explains how hiss body is for them. In other words, they must accept the sacrifice he is making on their behalf by taking the bread, which represents his body. Breaking the bread is symbolic of his broken body on the cross. Breaking bread together was also communal. In their world, food was scarce and people worked long and hard to grow it and preserve it through the winters. There were people you would share food with, and people who were a bit more distant. Sharing food, or "breaking bread together," established a level of relationship not shared with strangers.

Matthew records Jesus as saying, " . . . for this is my blood of the new covenant, which is poured out for many for the remission of sins."

Mark records Jesus as saying, "This is my blood of the new covenant, which is poured out for many."

Luke records Jesus taking a second cup and saying, "This cup is the new covenant in my blood, which is poured out for you."

The fact that Luke recorded Jesus drinking a cup before and after the bread is actually in line with Passover custom. In modern Passover meals, there are four cups of wine taken at different points in the meal.

John emphasizes the betrayal and service rather than the bread and wine. In John's account, Jesus washed the disciples' feet and taught them that they should be servants. Matthew, Mark, and Luke are demonstrating that Jesus laid down his life and gave his body and blood to save us from our sins. We should sacrifice in our own lives to serve and give to others.

4. Why did John's account leave out the institution of Communion?

John chose to emphasize the selflessness of Jesus and the power of service contrasted with the selfishness of the betrayal.

In Matthew, Mark, and Luke, giving the bread was communal. Giving the bread to the disciples created a level of relationship not shared with everyone.

In contrast, in John's account, giving the bread to Judas was an indictment of his guilt. In John, the act of giving bread was the opposite of communal. It excluded Judas.

5. What did Jesus mean when he said the cup is the new covenant in his blood?

Genesis 15

[1]After these things the word of the Lord came to Abram in a vision, saying, "Don't be afraid, Abram. I am your shield, your exceedingly great reward."

[2]Abram said, "Lord[93] Yahweh, what will you give me, since I go childless, and he who will inherit my estate is Eliezer of Damascus?" [3]Abram said, "Behold, to me you have given no seed: and, behold, one born in my house is my heir."

[4]Behold, the word of the Lord came to him, saying, "This man will not be your heir, but he who will come out of your own body will be your heir."

[5]The Lord brought him outside, and said, "Look now toward the sky, and count the stars, if you are able to count them." He said to Abram, "So shall your seed be." [6]He believed in the Lord; and he reckoned it to him for righteousness.

---

[93]   15:2 The word translated "Lord" is "Adonai."

⁷He said to him, "I am the Lord who brought you out of Ur of the Chaldees, to give you this land to inherit it."

⁸He said, "Lord Yahweh, how will I know that I will inherit it?"

⁹He said to him, "Bring me a heifer three years old, a female goat three years old, a ram three years old, a turtledove, and a young pigeon." ¹⁰He brought him all of these, and divided them in the middle, and laid each half opposite the other; but he didn't divide the birds. ¹¹The birds of prey came down on the carcasses, and Abram drove them away.

¹²When the sun was going down, a deep sleep fell on Abram. Now terror and great darkness fell on him. ¹³He said to Abram, "Know for sure that your seed will live as foreigners in a land that is not theirs, and will serve them. They will afflict them four hundred years. ¹⁴I will also judge that nation, whom they will serve. Afterward they will come out with great wealth, ¹⁵but you will go to your fathers in peace. You will be buried in a good old age. ¹⁶In the fourth generation they will come here again, for the iniquity of the Amorite is not yet full." ¹⁷It came to pass that, when the sun went down, and it was dark, behold, a smoking furnace, and a flaming torch passed between these pieces. ¹⁸In that day the Lord made a covenant with Abram, saying, "To your seed I have given this land, from the river of Egypt to the great river, the river Euphrates: ¹⁹the Kenites, the Kenizzites, the Kadmonites, ²⁰the Hittites, the Perizzites, the Rephaim, ²¹the Amorites, the Canaanites, the Girgashites, and the Jebusites."

In Genesis 15:7, God promised to give Abraham's descendants the land he was on. Abraham asked God how he could know that was true. In Genesis 15:9-21, God established a covenant with Abraham using the blood of a heifer, goat, and ram. A verse in Jeremiah tells us why the animals were cut in two and why God passed between the pieces in the form of a torch and smoking pot.

Jeremiah 34:18

[18]I will give the men who have transgressed my covenant, who have not performed the words of the covenant which they made before me, when they cut the calf in two and passed between its parts;

In Jeremiah, God was angry because the Israelites agreed to free their slaves and created a covenant to do it but later broke the covenant by retaining their slaves. A covenant made with blood means, "If I break the terms of this agreement, then the blood spilled to establish this covenant should be my blood."

In the time of Moses, God made a covenant with the Israelites. God made a sacred agreement to bless and protect the Israelites if they obeyed his commandments.

Exodus 24:4-8

[4]Moses wrote all the words of the Lord, and rose up early in the morning, and built an altar under the mountain, and twelve pillars for the twelve tribes of Israel. [5]He sent young men of the children of Israel, who offered burnt offerings and sacrificed peace offerings of cattle to the Lord. [6]Moses took half of the blood and put it in basins, and half of the blood he sprinkled on the altar. [7]He took the book of the covenant and read it in the hearing of the people, and they said, "All that the Lord has spoken will we do, and be obedient."

[8]Moses took the blood, and sprinkled it on the people, and said, "Look, this is the blood of the covenant, which the Lord has made with you concerning all these words."

The Old Covenant, or the Mosaic Covenant, was a sacred agreement between God and the people of Israel. According to this covenant, if the Israelites obeyed all the laws and commandments of God, God would be their God, and they would be his people and enjoy his blessing, favor, and protection. Sin is defined as breaking a commandment of God and, therefore, breaking the Old Covenant. Righteousness is defined as obeying the commandments of God. The blood of this covenant was from the cattle offered in sacrifice that Moses took and sprinkled on the altar and the people.

By the time of Jeremiah the prophet, the descendants of Israel had forgotten the covenant and rejected God to such a degree that God punished them by conquest and exile. In contrast to a covenant that required keeping the law, Jeremiah prophesied the coming of a new covenant with God.

Jeremiah 31:31-34

[31]Behold, the days come, says the Lord, that I will make a new covenant with the house of Israel, and with the house of Judah: [32]not according to the covenant that I made with their fathers in the day that I took them by the hand to bring them out of the land of Egypt; which my covenant they broke, although I was a husband to them, says the Lord. [33]But this is the covenant that I will make with the house of Israel after those days, says the Lord: I will put my law in their inward parts, and in their heart will I write it; and I will be their God, and they shall be my people: [34]and they shall teach no more every man his neighbor, and every man his brother, saying, Know the Lord; for they shall all know me, from their least to their greatest, says the Lord: for I will forgive their iniquity, and their sin will I remember no more.

The book of Hebrews in the New Testament explains the concept of the New Covenant and the blood of Christ.

Hebrews 9:11-15

[11]But Christ having come as a high priest of the coming good things, through the greater and more perfect tabernacle, not made with hands, that is to say, not of this creation, [12]nor yet through the blood of goats and calves, but through his own blood, entered in once for all into the Holy Place, having obtained eternal redemption. [13]For if the blood of goats and bulls, and the ashes of a heifer sprinkling those who have been defiled, sanctify to the cleanness of the flesh: [14]how much more will the blood of Christ, who through the eternal Spirit offered himself without blemish to God, cleanse

your conscience from dead works to serve the living God? [15]For this reason he is the mediator of a new covenant, since a death has occurred for the redemption of the transgressions that were under the first covenant, that those who have been called may receive the promise of the eternal inheritance.

When Jesus took the cup at the Passover meal and said, " . . . This is my blood of the new covenant, which is poured out for many for the forgiveness of sins." He was declaring that the new covenant prophesied by Jeremiah was about to be consecrated.

Jesus commanded the disciples to do the same ritual in remembrance of him and so instituted the Lord's Supper, or Communion, where Christians in successive generations gather to share in the fellowship of a common meal and remember the blood poured out to create the New Covenant that forgives sin.

This new covenant is not based on keeping the law because no one can keep it (except Jesus). We cannot achieve righteousness by keeping the law. This is why the New Covenant includes power to achieve righteousness. God said he would put his Spirit in us to help us.

Ezekiel 36:24-37

[24]For I will take you from among the nations, and gather you out of all the countries, and will bring you into your own land. [25]I will sprinkle clean water on you, and you shall be clean: from all your filthiness, and from all your idols, will I cleanse you. [26]I will also give you a new heart, and I will put a new spirit within you; and I will take away the stony heart out of your flesh, and I will give you a heart of flesh. [27]I will put my Spirit within you, and cause you to walk in my statutes, and you shall keep my ordinances, and do them.

Joel 2:28-31

[28]"It will happen afterward, that I will pour out my Spirit on all flesh;

and your sons and your daughters will prophesy.

Your old men will dream dreams.

Your young men will see visions.

[29]And also on the servants and on the handmaids in those days,
I will pour out my Spirit.

[30]I will show wonders in the heavens and in the earth: blood, fire,
and pillars of smoke.

[31]The sun will be turned into darkness, and the moon into blood,
before the great and terrible day of the Lord comes.

The Old Covenant contained the commandments and the expectation to keep them. The New Covenant puts God's Spirit in our hearts to help us to walk in God's way. Christians are given a Spirit of love. If we walk in love, we do, by nature, the things required by the law. If we love God with all our heart, soul, mind, and strength, and love our neighbor as our self, we do the things required by God to be righteous by nature. Christians have a power that legalistic law-keepers never had.

Communion is a covenant meal. Christians establish a bond of fellowship with one another by sharing together in the covenant meal. Remembering the broken body and shed blood of Christ is remembering the covenant God made with his people (the followers of Christ) using the blood of Christ. The new covenant says that God will remember our sins no more. It replaces our hearts of stone and gives us a new heart and a new Spirit that empowers us to walk in righteousness. If you live your life with an attitude of love for God and people, you will do the things required by the law.

Mark 14:27-31

[27]Jesus said to them, "All of you will be made to stumble because of me tonight, for it is written, 'I will strike the shepherd, and the sheep will be scattered.'[94] [28]However, after I am raised up, I will go before you into Galilee."

[29]But Peter said to him, "Although all will be offended, yet I will not."

---

[94]   14:27 Zechariah 13:7

³⁰Jesus said to him, "Most certainly I tell you, that you today, even this night, before the rooster crows twice, you will deny me three times."

³¹But he spoke all the more, "If I must die with you, I will not deny you." They all said the same thing.

1. How did Jesus know what was going to happen?

As the Son of God, he knew from the prophecy in Zechariah 13:7 that the shepherd was about to be struck and the sheep were about to be scattered. He knew that Judas had it in his heart to betray him. He knew what was in the hearts of the religious leaders and that they were plotting to kill him.

2. Do you think Peter actually believed he would never deny Jesus?

Yes, Peter believed it at the time. When Peter was eating a Passover meal in an upper room surrounded by believers, the world looked a certain way. When you are sitting next to a fire, surrounded by Roman soldiers, the world looks completely different.

3. How do people pledge commitment to Jesus today and then deny him?

Many people claim to follow Jesus when surrounded by Christians but act completely different when people mock and ridicule God, Jesus, faith, and the church.

Mark 8:38

³⁸For whoever will be ashamed of me and of my words in this adulterous and sinful generation, the Son of Man also will be ashamed of him, when he comes in the glory of his Father with the holy angels."

This adulterous and sinful generation desperately needs people of faith to stand up and say, "I'm a Christian, a follower of Christ."

Mark 14:32-42

³²They came to a place which was named Gethsemane. He said to his disciples, "Sit here, while I pray." ³³He took with him Peter, James, and John, and began to be greatly troubled and distressed. ³⁴He said to them, "My soul is exceedingly sorrowful, even to death. Stay here, and watch."

³⁵He went forward a little, and fell on the ground, and prayed that, if it were possible, the hour might pass away from him. ³⁶He said, "Abba, Father, all things are possible to you. Please remove this cup from me. However, not what I desire, but what you desire."

³⁷He came and found them sleeping, and said to Peter, "Simon, are you sleeping? Couldn't you watch one hour? ³⁸Watch and pray, that you may not enter into temptation. The spirit indeed is willing, but the flesh is weak."

³⁹Again he went away, and prayed, saying the same words. ⁴⁰Again he returned, and found them sleeping, for their eyes were very heavy, and they didn't know what to answer him. ⁴¹He came the third time, and said to them, "Sleep on now, and take your rest. It is enough. The hour has come. Behold, the Son of Man is betrayed into the hands of sinners. ⁴²Arise, let us be going. Behold, he who betrays me is at hand."

1. **Why did Jesus command most of the disciples to sit in a certain spot and then take Peter, James, and John farther?**

Jesus needed to pray before the events of the night began to unfold. He posted the majority of the disciples in one spot, partly to keep watch like sentries and partly because he wanted to be alone in prayer. He took Peter, James, and John farther and posted them as guards, or sentries, to keep watch and give him a measure of protection while he pleaded with God.

2. **What was Jesus struggling with?**

Jesus had a choice. He could stop his murder. He could spare himself the pain, humiliation, suffering, and death. He could defeat his earthly enemies, but his spiritual enemy, Satan, would win. If he chose to let the prophecies be fulfilled, he would be falsely accused and sentenced to an unjust death. He would be beaten, ridiculed, humiliated, and crucified by Romans. He would die. In that death, he trusted God to raise him to life. He knew the prophecies also foretold of the resurrection. By giving his life, he would conquer death for all of his followers. The greatest problem in this world is death, and no one has an answer for it except Jesus. Through his choice to follow God's plan, death was conquered and resurrection replaced it. Now, the followers of Jesus have a covenant put in place with Jesus' own blood that says our sins will be forgiven and we will be God's people and he will be our God. The followers of Jesus will live with God in the resurrection. We know it because God never breaks a covenant.

3. Three times the sentries were found asleep at their posts. How are modern Christians like the disciples in Gethsemane?

The world is getting darker and darker. The betrayer and the forces of evil are advancing, and many Christians sleep. Many Christians either deny what is happening or see it but feel powerless to make changes. Many Christians are so tired from the activities of life that a little sleep seems good. Jesus told the disciples to watch and pray. Modern Christians need to be watching and praying.

Mark 14:43-53

> [43]Immediately, while he was still speaking, Judas, one of the twelve, came—and with him a multitude with swords and clubs, from the chief priests, the scribes, and the elders. [44]Now he who betrayed him had given them a sign, saying, "Whomever I will kiss, that is he. Seize him, and lead him away safely." [45]When he had come, immediately he came to him, and said, "Rabbi! Rabbi!" and kissed him. [46]They laid their hands on him, and seized him. [47]But a certain one of those who stood by drew his sword, and struck the servant of the high priest, and cut off his ear.

> [48]Jesus answered them, "Have you come out, as against a robber, with swords and clubs to seize me? [49]I was daily with you in the

temple teaching, and you didn't arrest me. But this is so that the Scriptures might be fulfilled."

[50]They all left him, and fled. [51]A certain young man followed him, having a linen cloth thrown around himself, over his naked body. The young men grabbed him, [52]but he left the linen cloth, and fled from them naked. [53]They led Jesus away to the high priest. All the chief priests, the elders, and the scribes came together with him.

Matthew 26:47-58

[47]While he was still speaking, behold, Judas, one of the twelve, came, and with him a great multitude with swords and clubs, from the chief priest and elders of the people. [48]Now he who betrayed him gave them a sign, saying, "Whoever I kiss, he is the one. Seize him." [49]Immediately he came to Jesus, and said, "Hail, Rabbi!" and kissed him.

[50]Jesus said to him, "Friend, why are you here?" Then they came and laid hands on Jesus, and took him. [51]Behold, one of those who were with Jesus stretched out his hand, and drew his sword, and struck the servant of the high priest, and struck off his ear. [52]Then Jesus said to him, "Put your sword back into its place, for all those who take the sword will die by the sword. [53]Or do you think that I couldn't ask my Father, and he would even now send me more than twelve legions of angels? [54]How then would the Scriptures be fulfilled that it must be so?"

[55]In that hour Jesus said to the multitudes, "Have you come out as against a robber with swords and clubs to seize me? I sat daily in the temple teaching, and you didn't arrest me. [56]But all this has happened, that the Scriptures of the prophets might be fulfilled."

Then all the disciples left him, and fled. [57]Those who had taken Jesus led him away to Caiaphas the high priest, where the scribes and the elders were gathered together. [58]But Peter followed him from a distance, to the court of the high priest, and entered in and sat with the officers, to see the end.

1. Why did Judas use a kiss to betray Jesus?

It was proper honor etiquette to approach Jesus first and greet him as the teacher and leader. It was natural for Judas to walk past the other disciples and walk straight to Jesus. In their culture, a kiss was a greeting and sign of friendship and affection. In this case, it was a crafty way to specifically identify Jesus from the others in the garden. Using a greeting reserved for friends as a way to identify and betray Jesus is the ultimate irony.

2. According to John 18:10, Peter was the disciple who cut off the servant's ear. Was fighting with a sword out of character for Peter?

As was discussed many times in this study, the disciples joined Jesus because they thought the Messiah was to be a military leader who conquered Rome and became the new king. Peter was a man of action and probably would have defended Jesus with his life.

3. What was Jesus really saying to Peter when he said he could call twelve legions of angels?

In Rome, a legion had up to 6,000 soldiers when fully manned. Imagine if Jesus had shown Peter 72,000 angels standing around that tiny group of henchmen. How small would Peter have felt? Jesus did not need Peter's sword. Jesus could have used Peter's support and prayers in the garden a few minutes earlier. Jesus would have been encouraged had Peter stood firm in the courtyard in the hours before dawn. But part of the suffering prophesied in the Old Testament was that Jesus would be deserted by his followers.

4. How do you think Peter felt when Jesus stopped him?

Peter probably felt confused and frustrated. Peter pledged his life to protect Jesus but Jesus was refusing help. Peter could not understand. His preconceived ideas were blinding him. Peter would rather face a squad of men with clubs and swords than stand in a courtyard and say, "Yes, I am a follower of Jesus." Peter did not understand that fighting in the spiritual realm was different. Taking a stand in the face of ridicule and maintaining faith when persecution is imminent is more powerful than a sword. Because Peter and the others did not have the things of God in mind but the things of men, they ran in confusion, leaving Jesus to the mob.

5. In Mark 14:51-52, there is a description of a young man who fled naked from the Romans. Who was that?

Because it is only recorded in the book of Mark, and Mark would have been a young man at the time, it is generally regarded that it was Mark, who authored the book. It seems like the kind of detail that would seem significant to the one involved.

6. In Matthew 26:58, it says Peter followed at a distance. How does this describe many Christians today?

It was safer and more comfortable for Peter to follow at a distance rather than risk arrest and possibly share in the fate of Jesus. Many modern Christians want to follow Jesus at a safe distance where they are comfortable.

Mark 14:54-65

[54]Peter had followed him from a distance, until he came into the court of the high priest. He was sitting with the officers, and warming himself in the light of the fire. [55]Now the chief priests and the whole council sought witnesses against Jesus to put him to death, and found none. [56]For many gave false testimony against him, and their testimony didn't agree with each other. [57]Some stood up, and gave false testimony against him, saying, [58]"We heard him say, 'I will destroy this temple that is made with hands, and in three days I will build another made without hands.'" [59]Even so, their testimony did not agree.

[60]The high priest stood up in the midst, and asked Jesus, "Have you no answer? What is it which these testify against you?" [61]But he stayed quiet, and answered nothing. Again the high priest asked him, "Are you the Christ, the Son of the Blessed?"

[62]Jesus said, "I am. You will see the Son of Man sitting at the right hand of Power, and coming with the clouds of the sky."

[63]The high priest tore his clothes, and said, "What further need have we of witnesses? [64]You have heard the blasphemy! What do you think?" They all condemned him to be worthy of death. [65]Some began to spit on him, and to cover his face, and to beat him with fists, and to tell him, "Prophesy!" The officers struck him with the palms of their hands.

1. **Why did the chief priests and council have such a hard time finding a reason to kill Jesus?**

He was innocent. He had not committed a sin, and there was no true charge against him.

2. **Jesus stayed silent for most of the questioning. What do you think would have happened had he never spoken?**

The council probably could not have sent him to Pilate. The Jews were not allowed to condemn and execute prisoners without the consent of the local Roman authorities. They needed a capital offense.

3. **What was the high priest asking when he asked, "Are you the Christ, the Son of the Blessed?"**

Psalm 2:1-12

[1]Why do the nations rage,
  and the peoples plot a vain thing?
[2]The kings of the earth take a stand,
  and the rulers take counsel together,
  against the Lord, and against his Anointed,[95] saying,
[3]"Let's break their bonds apart,
  and cast their cords from us."

---

[95] 2:2 The word "Anointed" is the same as the word for "Messiah" or "Christ."

[4]He who sits in the heavens will laugh.
   The Lord[96] will have them in derision.
[5]Then he will speak to them in his anger,
   and terrify them in his wrath:
[6]"Yet I have set my King on my holy hill of Zion."
   [7]I will tell of the decree.
The Lord said to me, "You are my son.
   Today I have become your father.
[8]Ask of me, and I will give the nations for your inheritance,
   the uttermost parts of the earth for your possession.
[9]You shall break them with a rod of iron.
   You shall dash them in pieces like a potter's vessel."
[10]Now therefore be wise, you kings.
   Be instructed, you judges of the earth.
[11]Serve the Lord with fear,
   and rejoice with trembling.
[12]Give sincere homage to the Son[97], lest he be angry, and you perish
      in the way,
   for his wrath will soon be kindled.
   Blessed are all those who take refuge in him.

The high priest was asking if Jesus was the Messiah, the Son of God? The theme in the book of Mark, the identity of Jesus, reaches a climax at this point. Jesus broke his silence and answered with the truth. Jesus claimed to be the Son of God.

The mock trial stopped because the high priest had what he wanted. Not only was it blasphemy for a mere man to claim to be the Son of God, but it also was treason to Rome. Of course, it was not blasphemy if it was true. The high priest had a preconceived idea that Jesus was a threat that needed to be eliminated. Jesus could be sent to Pilate with charges that this prisoner confessed to being seditious and planning to overthrow Rome.

---

[96]   2:4 The word translated "Lord" is "Adonai."
[97]   2:12 or, Kiss the son

4. What did the corrupt religious leaders, the "holy men," do when Jesus told the truth?

They beat Jesus. You will know them by their fruit.

Mark 14:66-72

> [66]As Peter was in the courtyard below, one of the maids of the high priest came, [67]and seeing Peter warming himself, she looked at him, and said, "You were also with the Nazarene, Jesus!"
>
> [68]But he denied it, saying, "I neither know, nor understand what you are saying." He went out on the porch, and the rooster crowed.
>
> [69]The maid saw him, and began again to tell those who stood by, "This is one of them." [70]But he again denied it. After a little while again those who stood by said to Peter, "You truly are one of them, for you are a Galilean, and your speech shows it." [71]But he began to curse, and to swear, "I don't know this man of whom you speak!" [72]The rooster crowed the second time. Peter remembered the word, how that Jesus said to him, "Before the rooster crows twice, you will deny me three times." When he thought about that, he wept.

1. Just a few hours earlier, Peter had pledged to never deny Jesus. In fact, Peter was ready to fight a mob with swords to defend Jesus. What happened that changed Peter and caused him to deny Jesus three times?

Fighting with a sword made sense to Peter. He understood revolution. He did not understand spiritual warfare. He did not yet know that taking a stand and holding to your beliefs is far more powerful than any sword. Peter had a preconceived idea that the Messiah could not die. It was barely even conceivable that the Messiah could be arrested. Peter probably reasoned that this was the start of the revolution. That was certainly what the chief priests were afraid of and why they arrested Jesus at night. Peter did not understand the tremendous spiritual implications of denying he was with Jesus.

Mark 8:38

³⁸For whoever will be ashamed of me and of my words in this adulterous and sinful generation, the Son of Man also will be ashamed of him, when he comes in the glory of his Father with the holy angels."

2. How do you think Peter felt when the rooster crowed?

It reminded him of what Jesus said. At that moment, he realized several things. Jesus prophesied what would happen, and it came to pass. Peter was willing to do the hard thing, fight to the death with a sword, but he failed in the easy thing, being identified with Jesus. Peter wept over his denial.

John 21:13-19

¹³Then Jesus came and took the bread, gave it to them, and the fish likewise. ¹⁴This is now the third time that Jesus was revealed to his disciples, after he had risen from the dead. ¹⁵So when they had eaten their breakfast, Jesus said to Simon Peter, "Simon, son of Jonah, do you love me more than these?"

He said to him, "Yes, Lord; you know that I have affection for you."

He said to him, "Feed my lambs." ¹⁶He said to him again a second time, "Simon, son of Jonah, do you love me?"

He said to him, "Yes, Lord; you know that I have affection for you."

He said to him, "Tend my sheep." ¹⁷He said to him the third time, "Simon, son of Jonah, do you have affection for me?"

Peter was grieved because he asked him the third time, "Do you have affection for me?" He said to him, "Lord, you know everything. You know that I have affection for you."

Jesus said to him, "Feed my sheep.

¹⁸Most certainly I tell you, when you were young, you dressed yourself, and walked where you wanted to. But when you are old, you will stretch out your hands, and another will dress you, and carry you where you don't want to go."

¹⁹Now he said this, signifying by what kind of death he would glorify God. When he had said this, he said to him, "Follow me."

John records what is considered the reinstatement of Peter. Peter, during the Passover meal and Communion, claimed to love Jesus more than the other disciples and claimed he would die before denying Jesus. Then he denied Jesus three times.

There is nothing here that suggests Peter is reinstated to a position of authority. It is clearly a message that even though someone declares undying love for Jesus, they can be forgiven and accepted back by Jesus if they repent.

The Greeks had four words for love that are often translated interchangeably with the one English word "love." In this case, two of the words are used. "Agape" is the Greek word for committed love. "Phileo" is the Greek word for the affection of friendship. The word phileo conveys less commitment than agape.

Jesus asked Peter, "Do you agape me?" He was asking, "Are you committed to me with undying love like you claimed?" Peter replied, "Yes, Lord, you know I phileo you." In essence he replied, "You know I am your friend." Jesus said, "Feed my lambs."

A second time, Jesus asked Peter, "Do you agape me?" Again, Peter replied, "You know I phileo you." Jesus said, "Tend my sheep."

The third time, Jesus did not use the word agape. He used the word phileo. Jesus said to Peter the third time, "Do you phileo me?" He was asking Peter, "Are you sure you are even my friend?" The text says Peter was grieved. Peter answered the third time, "Yes, you know all things, you know I (phileo you) am your friend."

Peter had learned not to overstate his commitment. This was a huge step in his personal growth.

This also teaches volumes about a relationship with Jesus. Commitment to Jesus is not a relationship we can put on the shelf six days a week and be "his friend" whenever it suits us. The question for Christians today is whether we are in a committed relationship of agape or just friends with Jesus when we want to be and it's not too embarrassing.

Chapter 15

Mark 15:1-15

¹Immediately in the morning, the chief priests, with the elders and scribes, and the whole council, held a consultation, and bound Jesus, and carried him away, and delivered him up to Pilate.

²Pilate asked him, "Are you the King of the Jews?"

He answered, "Yes, it is as you say."

³The chief priests accused him of many things. ⁴Pilate again asked him, "Have you no answer? See how many things they testify against you!"

⁵But Jesus made no further answer, so that Pilate marveled.

⁶Now at the feast, Pilate used to release one prisoner to them, whom ever they asked of him. ⁷There was one called Barabbas, imprisoned with those who had taken part in an insurrection and had committed murder in the insurrection. ⁸The multitude, crying aloud, began to ask him to do as he always did for them. ⁹Pilate answered them, saying, "Do you want me to release to you the King of the Jews?" ¹⁰For he knew that it was due to envy the chief priests had delivered him up. ¹¹But the chief priests stirred up the multitude to have Pilate release Barabbas to them instead. ¹²Pilate again asked them, "What then should I do to him whom you call the King of the Jews?"

[13]They cried out again, "Crucify him!"

[14]Pilate said to them, "Why, what evil has he done?"

But they cried out exceedingly, "Crucify him!"

[15]Pilate, wishing to please the multitude, released Barabbas to them, and had Jesus flogged and handed him over to be crucified.

1. Why did the Sanhedrin, the Jewish ruling council, hold a trial in the middle of the night?

It was against Roman law for the Jews to execute anyone, even a felon. The accused criminals had to be turned over and found guilty by the Romans. In this case, the Jews wanted to charge Jesus with sedition and treason against Rome, so he would get the death penalty.

They held the trial in the middle of the night to escape being seen by the people. The people loved Jesus and would never have tolerated a mock trial to condemn an innocent man. They would have rioted.

2. Jesus only answered one question or charge. Why?

Had Jesus not answered any accusation, Pilate may have dismissed the proceedings and let Jesus go. He answered the one question that mattered, "Who are you?" Again, that is what the book of Mark is about. Jesus clearly stated that he was the king of the Jews. With all the talk of the Messiah coming to save Israel and take his place as King of Kings and Lord of Lords, acknowledging that he was king of the Jews was claiming to be the Messiah. There were so many Jews talking about revolting against Rome that this claim was at least seditious, if not treason. Jesus did not need to answer any other charge. His one answer was enough to be sentenced to die.

3. Did Pilate think Jesus was guilty?

In the Gospels, Pilate appears to know the truth but fails to live up to it. He is the best example of someone caving in to peer pressure. He went with the crowd.

4. **How do people repeat Pilate's mistake today? What do people know but fail to live up to? How do people give in to the crowd today?**

They know the truth about God and Jesus but try to ignore what they know is true and deny any responsibility.

The crowd today says it is "lame" to be a Christian. Many Christians are closet Christians. They are ashamed to be identified with Jesus.

Pilate was afraid of the crowd like many people today are afraid of the crowd.

Pilate wanted to be liked and respected. We sometimes have to choose who we want to like us and respect us.

5. **Who was Barabbas, and why was he in prison?**

Barabbas was one of the Jews trying to fight and overthrow Roman occupation. He had taken part in an insurrection against Rome. People were murdered.

6. **Imagine what it was like that morning for Barabbas.**

Barabbas knew he was going to die. He and his comrades had killed some Romans. He probably did not sleep that last night. He wondered what suffering he would endure as death approached. Then he heard footsteps. Soldiers were coming for him. The prison door was unlocked, and a soldier yelled at him, "Get up. You're free by the immeasurable grace of our merciful king, Pilate." Barabbas may not have believed the guard. They dragged him out of the prison, and he fully expected to be stabbed with the sword. They might have brought him in front of Pilate and the crowd. Maybe he saw Jesus being flogged and wondered what was going on. There would have been a grand announcement about the limitless mercy of Pilate, and Barabbas would be released.

7. **At some point, someone told Barabbas what happened. How would you have felt if you were Barabbas? How do you think Barabbas felt when he learned that Jesus took his place?**

Barabbas may have felt nothing toward Jesus. He may have felt extreme gratitude that he was released but not cared at all that Jesus took the cross meant for him. On the other hand, Barabbas may have felt deep gratitude toward Jesus for taking his place. Barabbas knew he was guilty and deserved that cross. Someone may have told him that Jesus was innocent. An innocent man was taking his place. How do you feel? You are Barabbas in this story. Jesus took your place.

Barabbas illustrates the two main reactions people have. They are either indifferent toward Jesus dying on the cross and just happy to be living now, or they know they deserve to be on that cross and an innocent man should not have died for them.

Barabbas represents each person forgiven by the blood of Christ. You are Barabbas in this story. Barabbas was a sinner. He was imprisoned because of his sin. He was guilty and deserved to die for his sin. Jesus was innocent, yet he died on the cross meant for Barabbas. This is a metaphor, symbolizing Jesus taking the place of each Christian condemned by sin and freed because of his death in their place. You should feel the same love and gratitude that Barabbas should have felt.

Mark 15:16–20

> [16]The soldiers led him away within the court, which is the Praetorium; and they called together the whole cohort. [17]They clothed him with purple, and weaving a crown of thorns, they put it on him. [18]They began to salute him, "Hail, King of the Jews!" [19]They struck his head with a reed, and spat on him, and bowing their knees, did homage to him. [20]When they had mocked him, they took the purple off of him, and put his own garments on him. They led him out to crucify him.

1. Why did a group of men brutalize, beat, and humiliate Jesus?

The easy answer is to fulfill prophecy. We will see that in the next section. These men were angry and hated Jesus because he was Jewish and because a mere Jew claimed to be better than them.

It is not surprising that Roman soldiers treated Jesus this way. The real surprise is that the religious leaders, members of the Sanhedrin, treated Jesus the same way. They were no better than these men.

2. **How did these men feel in the afterlife when they were ushered into the throne room of the universe and saw Jesus sitting at the right hand of God?**

It would be hard to describe the utter despair, shame, guilt, and hopelessness one would feel after mocking the Son of God and then appearing before him to be judged.

Mark 15:21-32

[21]They compelled one passing by, coming from the country, Simon of Cyrene, the father of Alexander and Rufus, to go with them, that he might bear his cross. [22]They brought him to the place called Golgotha, which is, being interpreted, "The place of a skull." [23]They offered him wine mixed with myrrh to drink, but he didn't take it.

[24]Crucifying him, they parted his garments among them, casting lots on them, what each should take. [25]It was the third hour,[98] and they crucified him. [26]The superscription of his accusation was written over him, "THE KING OF THE JEWS." [27]With him they crucified two robbers; one on his right hand, and one on his left. [28]The Scripture was fulfilled, which says, "He was numbered with transgressors."[99]

[29]Those who passed by blasphemed him, wagging their heads, and saying, "Ha! You who destroy the temple, and build it in three days, [30]save yourself, and come down from the cross!"

[31]Likewise, also the chief priests mocking among themselves with the scribes said, "He saved others. He can't save himself. [32]Let the

---

[98] 15:25 9:00 A. M.
[99] 15:28 NU omits verse 28

Christ, the King of Israel, now come down from the cross, that we may see and believe him.[100]" Those who were crucified with him insulted him.

1. Simon was forced to carry the cross for Jesus? Why?

At this point, Jesus had been beaten so severely he did not have the strength to carry the cross.

2. How would you feel if you had to carry Jesus' cross for him?

Hopefully, honored. We all have that opportunity today.

(Note: The discussion could move to ways we can carry the cross today.)

3. Why did Jesus refuse the wine that was mixed with myrrh?

Jesus may have refused the wine because he promised his disciples he would not drink it again until he drank it anew with them in the kingdom of God (Communion).

4. What were the soldiers doing at the foot of the cross?

<u>**John 19:23-24**</u>

> [23]Then the soldiers, when they had crucified Jesus, took his garments and made four parts, to every soldier a part; and also the coat. Now the coat was without seam, woven from the top throughout. [24]Then they said to one another, "Let's not tear it, but cast lots for it to decide whose it will be," that the Scripture might be fulfilled, which says,
>
> > "They parted my garments among them.
> > For my cloak they cast lots."[101]

---

[100]   15:32 TR omits "him"
[101]   19:24 Psalm 22:18

Therefore the soldiers did these things.

The soldiers cast lots for his clothing. Casting lots was something similar to using dice to determine who might receive something by chance.

As John describes, it happened to fulfill Old Testament prophecy in Psalm 22.

The metaphor here is that men were playing games at the foot of the cross during the most profound event in human history. Much could be said about people today playing games at the foot of the cross.

5. Why did the Roman soldiers put a sign on the cross saying, "King of the Jews?"

The Jews were constantly talking about revolt and revolution. Many Zealots had tried to start uprisings, as in the case of Barabbas. For the Romans, the sign served the purpose of deterrence. It meant that this man was not being crucified because he was a thief or common criminal like the other two men dying that day. It said, "This is how Rome deals with revolutionaries."

There may have also been an element of spite in putting the sign over Jesus. According to John, the Chief Priest and some Jews complained to Pilate that the sign should read, "This man claimed to be king of the Jews." As it was, it made the religious leaders look like they killed their own king.

6. Why did the people standing by hurl insults?

Matthew 27:39-44

> [39]Those who passed by blasphemed him, wagging their heads, [40]and saying, "You who destroy the temple, and build it in three days, save yourself! If you are the Son of God, come down from the cross!"

[41]Likewise the chief priests also mocking, with the scribes, the Pharisees,[102] and the elders, said, [42]"He saved others, but he can't save himself. If he is the King of Israel, let him come down from the cross now, and we will believe in him. [43]He trusts in God. Let God deliver him now, if he wants him; for he said, 'I am the Son of God.'" [44]The robbers also who were crucified with him cast on him the same reproach.

The insults were prophesied in great detail and fulfilled in this moment (see the next section for a description of the prophecies). It also shows the depth of depravity reached by the religious leaders and their followers. They were gloating that they had won. It is very much something Satan might say at the foot of the cross. The Jewish leaders were completely depraved. Matthew comments that even the robbers were insulting Jesus to show that the religious leaders were not much different than the criminals.

Luke 23:39–43

[39]One of the criminals who was hanged insulted him, saying, "If you are the Christ, save yourself and us!"

[40]But the other answered, and rebuking him said, "Don't you even fear God, seeing you are under the same condemnation? [41]And we indeed justly, for we receive the due reward for our deeds, but this man has done nothing wrong." [42]He said to Jesus, "Lord, remember me when you come into your kingdom."

[43]Jesus said to him, "Assuredly I tell you, today you will be with me in Paradise."

While Matthew and Mark recorded that both criminals hurled insults, there came a point when one of the criminals repented and chose a different course. He seems to have come to his senses as death approached. His statement is a statement of faith. He believed in Jesus. Jesus responded that his faith would save him.

---

[102]   27:41 TR omits "the Pharisees"

The afterlife is divided into four places. Before the resurrection, the afterlife is referred to as either the Hadean world or Hades, the underworld. Hades is spoken of as two places, Paradise and Tartarus. In Luke 16:23, the rich man woke up in hell, or Tartarus, in agony. Disembodied spirits are conscious and waiting for Judgement Day, when all will be resurrected, including the believers and the unbelievers. After Judgement Day, there are two realms of eternal existence, heaven and hell. Everyone will have an eternal body as part of the resurrection, but those who came from Tartarus will enter hell and those who wait in Paradise will enter heaven.

Mark 15:33-41

[33]When the sixth hour[103] had come, there was darkness over the whole land until the ninth hour.[104] [34]At the ninth hour Jesus cried with a loud voice, saying, "Eloi, Eloi, lama sabachthani?" which is, being interpreted, "My God, my God, why have you forsaken me?"[105]

[35]Some of those who stood by, when they heard it, said, "Behold, he is calling Elijah."

[36]One ran, and filling a sponge full of vinegar, put it on a reed, and gave it to him to drink, saying, "Let him be. Let's see whether Elijah comes to take him down."

[37]Jesus cried out with a loud voice, and gave up the spirit. [38]The veil of the temple was torn in two from the top to the bottom. [39]When the centurion, who stood by opposite him, saw that he cried out like this and breathed his last, he said, "Truly this man was the Son of God!"

[40]There were also women watching from afar, among whom were both Mary Magdalene, and Mary the mother of James the less and

---

[103] 15:33 or, noon
[104] 15:33 3:00 PM
[105] 15:34 Psalm 22:1

of Joses, and Salome; [41]who, when he was in Galilee, followed him, and served him; and many other women who came up with him to Jerusalem.

1. Did Jesus believe God had forsaken him? Why did he cry out with that statement?

There are two major schools of thought. One says that Jesus took on the sins of the world. The penalty from sin is death, or separation from God. In order for Jesus to actually take the punishment for our sins, he had to be separated from God. This school of thought says that when all the sin in the world came upon Jesus, God turned his face away and Jesus suffered utter separation from God—something he had never known before.

The other school of thought says that Jesus was quoting Psalm 22. King David wrote Psalm 22 one thousand years before their fulfillment in the crucifixion of Jesus. There are amazing prophecies that are fulfilled by the enemies of Jesus at his crucifixion. They would have never said what did if they had remembered these prophecies.

(Note: Underlines are supplied to draw attention to words and actions of the enemies of Jesus.)

Psalm 22:1-31

[1]My God, my God, why have you forsaken me?
Why are you so far from helping me, and from the words of my
    groaning?
[2]My God, I cry in the daytime, but you don't answer;
    in the night season, and am not silent.
[3]But you are holy,
    you who inhabit the praises of Israel.
[4]Our fathers trusted in you.
    They trusted, and you delivered them.
[5]They cried to you, and were delivered.
    They trusted in you, and were not disappointed.
[6]But I am a worm, and no man;
    a reproach of men, and despised by the people.

⁷All those who see me mock me.
>   They insult me with their lips. They shake their heads, saying,
>   ⁸"He trusts in the Lord;
>   let him deliver him.
>   Let him rescue him, since he delights in him."

⁹But you brought me out of the womb.
>   You made me trust at my mother's breasts.

¹⁰I was thrown on you from my mother's womb.
>   You are my God since my mother bore me.

¹¹Don't be far from me, for trouble is near.
>   For there is none to help.

¹²Many bulls have surrounded me.
>   Strong bulls of Bashan have encircled me.

¹³They open their mouths wide against me,
>   lions tearing prey and roaring.

¹⁴I am poured out like water.
>   All my bones are out of joint.

My heart is like wax;
>   it is melted within me.

¹⁵My strength is dried up like a potsherd.
>   My tongue sticks to the roof of my mouth.

You have brought me into the dust of death.

¹⁶For dogs have surrounded me.
>   A company of evildoers have enclosed me.
>   They have pierced my hands and feet.[106]

¹⁷I can count all of my bones.

They look and stare at me.

¹⁸They divide my garments among them.
>   They cast lots for my clothing.

¹⁹But don't be far off, Lord.
>   You are my help: hurry to help me.

²⁰Deliver my soul from the sword,
>   my precious life from the power of the dog.

²¹Save me from the lion's mouth!

---

[106] 22:16 So Dead Sea Scrolls. Masoretic Text reads, "Like a lion, they pin my hands and feet."

Yes, from the horns of the wild oxen, you have answered me.
²²I will declare your name to my brothers.

In the midst of the assembly, I will praise you.
²³You who fear the Lord, praise him!

All you descendants of Jacob, glorify him!

Stand in awe of him, all you descendants of Israel!
²⁴For he has not despised nor abhorred the affliction of the
afflicted,

Neither has he hidden his face from him;

but when he cried to him, he heard.
²⁵Of you comes my praise in the great assembly.

I will pay my vows before those who fear him.
²⁶The humble shall eat and be satisfied.

They shall praise the Lord who seek after him.

Let your hearts live forever.
²⁷All the ends of the earth shall remember and turn to the Lord.

All the relatives of the nations shall worship before you.
²⁸For the kingdom is the Lord's.

He is the ruler over the nations.
²⁹All the rich ones of the earth shall eat and worship.

All those who go down to the dust shall bow before him,

even he who can't keep his soul alive.
³⁰Posterity shall serve him.

Future generations shall be told about the Lord.
³¹They shall come and shall declare his righteousness to a people
that shall be born,

for he has done it.

All the verses of this Psalm can apply to Jesus without twisting the meaning.

Which school of thought accurately answers why Jesus cried out quoting Psalm 22:1? Perhaps both.

2. **At the moment of Jesus' death, verse 38 says the temple curtain was torn in two from top to bottom. What did this symbolize?**

The Jews built the Temple as a place for their God to dwell with them. There was a huge curtain in the Temple that separated the Holy of Holies from the rest of the courtyards where worshippers could go. The Holy of Holies was where God lived. Only the high priest was allowed to enter the Holy of Holies once a year to offer sacrifice for the sins of the people. The curtain was a separation between God and the people. The death of Jesus satisfied the debt of sin, so the curtain separating God from his people was torn from the top to the bottom. Had it been torn from bottom to top, it would appear to have been done by man. Tearing from top to bottom signified that it was torn by God. Because of Jesus, the separation between God and man was removed.

3. What is so significant about the Roman centurion's assertion, "Truly this man was the Son of God!"

The theme of the book of Mark is the identity of Jesus. The disciples struggled with who Jesus was. They knew he was the Messiah, the Christ, but they did not understand what that meant. The religious leaders were corrupt and could not accept the identity of Jesus. The people who should have known who Jesus was missed it so completely that they had him murdered. It took a Roman centurion to get it right. As scholarship suggests, the book of Mark is probably the preaching of Peter in the city of Rome. This message was probably originally delivered to a Roman audience. The fact that the Roman centurion testifies to the identity of Jesus would have been significant to that audience.

4. Why mention the women who were at the crucifixion?

Mainly because the men seemed to be absent. Except for John, who was there with Mary, Jesus' mother, the disciples seem to be conspicuously absent.

Mark 15:42-47

42When evening had now come, because it was the Preparation Day, that is, the day before the Sabbath, 43Joseph of Arimathaea, a prominent council member who also himself was looking for the kingdom of God, came. He boldly went in to Pilate, and asked for Jesus' body. [44]Pilate marveled if he were already dead; and summoning the centurion, he asked him whether he had been dead long. [45]When he found out from the centurion, he granted the body to Joseph. [46]He bought a linen cloth, and taking him down, wound him in the linen cloth, and laid him in a tomb which had been cut out of a rock. He rolled a stone against the door of the tomb. [47]Mary Magdalene and Mary, the mother of Joses, saw where he was laid.

John 19:31–42

[31]Therefore the Jews, because it was the Preparation Day, so that the bodies wouldn't remain on the cross on the Sabbath (for that Sabbath was a special one), asked of Pilate that their legs might be broken, and that they might be taken away. [32]Therefore the soldiers came, and broke the legs of the first, and of the other who was crucified with him; [33]but when they came to Jesus, and saw that he was already dead, they didn't break his legs. [34]However one of the soldiers pierced his side with a spear, and immediately blood and water came out. [35]He who has seen has testified, and his testimony is true. He knows that he tells the truth, that you may believe. [36]For these things happened, that the Scripture might be fulfilled, "A bone of him will not be broken."[107] [37]Again another Scripture says, "They will look on him whom they pierced."[108]

[38]After these things, Joseph of Arimathaea, being a disciple of Jesus, but secretly for fear of the Jews, asked of Pilate that he might take away Jesus' body. Pilate gave him permission. He came therefore and took away his body. [39]Nicodemus, who at first came to Jesus by night, also came bringing a mixture of myrrh and aloes, about a hundred Roman pounds.[109] [40]So they took Jesus' body, and bound it in linen cloths with the spices, as the custom of the Jews is to bury. [41]Now in the place where he was crucified there was a garden. In the garden was a new tomb

---

[107] 19:36 Exodus 12:46; Numbers 9:12; Psalm 34:20

[108] 19:37 Zechariah 12:10

[109] 19:39 100 Roman pounds of 12 ounces each, or about 72 pounds, or 33 Kilograms.

in which no man had ever yet been laid. ⁴²Then because of the Jews' Preparation Day (for the tomb was near at hand) they laid Jesus there.

1. How were Peter and Joseph of Arimathaea similar and different?

Peter was a disciple of Jesus publicly while Joseph was a secret disciple. But even as a secret disciple, Joseph was willing to go boldly before Pilate and ask for Jesus' body.

2. Are secret disciples of Jesus accepted today?

No, Peter's denial of Jesus teaches us that secret disciples are not accepted. People must identify with Jesus as Lord and Savior. Jesus explained this in Mark 8:38.

Mark 8:38

³⁸For whoever will be ashamed of me and of my words in this adulterous and sinful generation, the Son of Man also will be ashamed of him, when he comes in the glory of his Father with the holy angels."

3. Was Jesus really dead?

Roman centurions knew what death looked like. The enemies of Jesus were there to make sure Jesus was dead. John's testimony that water and blood gushed from the wound in his side, as well as the testimony of all the Gospel writers, affirms that Jesus was dead.

Chapter 16

¹When the Sabbath was past, Mary Magdalene, and Mary the mother of James, and Salome, bought spices, that they might come and anoint him. ²Very early on the first day of the week, they came to the tomb when the sun had risen. ³They were saying among themselves, "Who will roll away the stone from the door of the tomb for us?" ⁴for it was very big. Looking up, they saw that the stone was rolled back.

⁵Entering into the tomb, they saw a young man sitting on the right side, dressed in a white robe, and they were amazed. ⁶He said to them, "Don't be amazed. You seek Jesus, the Nazarene, who has been crucified. He has risen. He is not here. Behold, the place where they laid him! ⁷But go, tell his disciples and Peter, 'He goes before you into Galilee. There you will see him, as he said to you.'"

⁸They went out,[110] and fled from the tomb, for trembling and astonishment had come on them. They said nothing to anyone; for they were afraid.

1. **Who are the women mentioned in verse 1, and what do their actions reveal?**

---

[110] 16:8 TR adds "quickly"

The women are the same women mentioned in Mark 15:40 that watched the crucifixion from a distance.

They believed they would find the dead body of Jesus. They brought spices to anoint the body for a proper burial.

They believed that God would provide a way. On the road to the tomb, they talked about who would move the stone from the tomb. Even without a defined way to open the tomb, they believed it would happen. Indeed, God did provide a way. An angel moved the stone and rendered the guards unconscious.

2. Who was the young man dressed in a white robe?

Matthew 28:1-10

> [1]Now after the Sabbath, as it began to dawn on the first day of the week, Mary Magdalene and the other Mary came to see the tomb. [2]Behold, there was a great earthquake, for an angel of the Lord descended from the sky, and came and rolled away the stone from the door, and sat on it. [3]His appearance was like lightning, and his clothing white as snow. [4]For fear of him, the guards shook, and became like dead men. [5]The angel answered the women, "Don't be afraid, for I know that you seek Jesus, who has been crucified. [6]He is not here, for he has risen, just like he said. Come, see the place where the Lord was lying. [7]Go quickly and tell his disciples, 'He has risen from the dead, and behold, he goes before you into Galilee; there you will see him.' Behold, I have told you."
>
> [8]They departed quickly from the tomb with fear and great joy, and ran to bring his disciples word. [9]As they went to tell his disciples, behold, Jesus met them, saying, "Rejoice!"

They came and took hold of his feet, and worshiped him.

[10]Then Jesus said to them, "Don't be afraid. Go tell my brothers[111] that they should go into Galilee, and there they will see me."

According to Matthew, the messenger announcing the resurrection was an angel of God. The resurrection was announced by an angel and confirmed by Jesus himself.

3. Why were guards posted outside the tomb?

Matthew 27:62-66

[62]Now on the next day, which was the day after the Preparation Day, the chief priests and the Pharisees were gathered together to Pilate, [63]saying, "Sir, we remember what that deceiver said while he was still alive: 'After three days I will rise again.' [64]Command therefore that the tomb be made secure until the third day, lest perhaps his disciples come at night and steal him away, and tell the people, 'He is risen from the dead;' and the last deception will be worse than the first."

[65]Pilate said to them, "You have a guard. Go, make it as secure as you can." [66]So they went with the guard and made the tomb secure, sealing the stone.

The enemies of Jesus wanted to prevent any rumors. They did not realize that they were only adding authenticity to the resurrection claim. By securing the tomb and preventing anyone from stealing the body, they added a layer of assurance that the resurrection was authentic.

4. Why is authenticating the resurrection so important?

If Jesus was raised from the dead, Christianity is true. If Jesus is still dead, Christianity is a hoax.

---

[111] 28:10 The word for "brothers" here may be also correctly translated "brothers and sisters" or "siblings."

The premise of Christianity is that Jesus is the Son of God who came to die for our sins and pay the penalty for them so that death would have no mastery over us. Through this, we can live with God for ever in heaven. Sin and death were conquered in the resurrection.

The biggest problem that people face is death. No other world religion has an answer for death. Jesus is the answer. His resurrection means we can be resurrected. His life after death means we can have life after death. His resurrection confirms his identity as the Son of God and confirms his teachings and authority are from God.

5. Unbelievers claim that the disciples stole the body of Jesus. How do we know this is not true?

Matthew 28:11-15

> [11]Now while they were going, behold, some of the guards came into the city, and told the chief priests all the things that had happened. [12]When they were assembled with the elders, and had taken counsel, they gave a large amount of silver to the soldiers, [13]saying, "Say that his disciples came by night, and stole him away while we slept. [14]If this comes to the governor's ears, we will persuade him and make you free of worry." [15]So they took the money and did as they were told. This saying was spread abroad among the Jews, and continues until this day.

The main evidence we have is the testimony of the disciples who walked with Jesus and witnessed his resurrection. If they stole the body and perpetuated a hoax, they died for their hoax in the most gruesome ways. Peter was crucified in Rome upside down. The other disciples were martyred for their faith. John was the only one of the Twelve to live to an old age. Ancient accounts say that John was dropped into a vat of boiling oil to silence him but nothing happened to him. It disturbed his persecutors, so they exiled him to the Island of Patmos, where he eventually wrote the book of Revelation.

If Christianity was a hoax, at least one of the disciples would have recanted to save their life. The enemies of Jesus would have paraded a disciple to every city in the Roman Empire to declare the hoax.

That it never happened. Each of the disciples went to gruesome deaths maintaining the truth of the resurrection.

Matthew 16:9-20

[9]Now when he had risen early on the first day of the week, he appeared first to Mary Magdalene, from whom he had cast out seven demons. [10]She went and told those who had been with him, as they mourned and wept. [11]When they heard that he was alive, and had been seen by her, they disbelieved. [12]After these things he was revealed in another form to two of them, as they walked, on their way into the country. [13]They went away and told it to the rest. They didn't believe them, either.

[14]Afterward he was revealed to the eleven themselves as they sat at the table, and he rebuked them for their unbelief and hardness of heart, because they didn't believe those who had seen him after he had risen. [15]He said to them, "Go into all the world, and preach the Good News to the whole creation. [16]He who believes and is baptized will be saved; but he who disbelieves will be condemned. [17]These signs will accompany those who believe: in my name they will cast out demons; they will speak with new languages; [18]they will take up serpents; and if they drink any deadly thing, it will in no way hurt them; they will lay hands on the sick, and they will recover."

[19]So then the Lord[112], after he had spoken to them, was received up into heaven, and sat down at the right hand of God. [20]They went out, and preached everywhere, the Lord working with them, and confirming the word by the signs that followed. Amen.

(Note: Many biblical scholars have questioned the authenticity of verses 9-20.

Arguments against the authenticity of this section include manuscript evidence, literary evidence, and word counts.

---

[112] 16:19 NA adds "Jesus"

Regarding manuscript evidence, the two oldest complete manuscripts of Mark [Sinaiticus and Vaticanus from the fourth century] end with Mark 16:8. A few other manuscripts, which were copied after these, have a shorter ending after verse 8 that seems to have been added in an attempt to bring the story to a close.

Regarding literary evidence, verse 9 does not flow with verse 8. It seems awkward. Others find the apparent emphasis on baptism and miraculous gifts inconsistent with their liberal theology.

Regarding word counts, there have been suggestions that the writer of verses 9-20 used a slightly different vocabulary and style, although this train of thought is so weak it has failed to gain acceptance.

Evidence that Mark 16:9-20 is valid and original includes patristic quotations from the second century, literary considerations, and chiastic considerations.

Regarding patristic quotations, a number of letters from church fathers in the second century quote parts of Mark 16:9-20. That would have been difficult to do if they were not there. The evidence clearly shows that Mark 16:9-20 was written at the time of the second century [A.D. 140 and A.D. 172]. The earliest copies of Mark were written on scrolls with columns of text. It is very conceivable that the last column of text was broken off and lost on certain copies by the fourth century.

Literary considerations regarding the authenticity of Mark 16:9-20 include whether Mark 16:8 is a good ending.

Mark 16:8

⁸*They went out,*[113] *and fled from the tomb, for trembling and astonishment had come on them. They said nothing to anyone; for they were afraid.*

It is difficult to believe that Mark chose to end the story of his Lord with verse 8.

Finally, chiastic or structural considerations regarding the authenticity of this section are based on the fact that Mark began the book with a fifteen-verse introduction

---

[113]   16:8 TR adds "quickly"

that talks about preaching the Gospel, or Good News, and the baptism of Jesus. It seems structurally appropriate that he would have a concluding section. The concluding section is very similar to the introduction. It is chiastically complete to end with preaching the Good News and the baptism of the followers of Jesus.)

1. **Verse 11 says that Mary Magdalene told the disciples that Jesus was alive, but they didn't believe her Why?**

They knew Jesus was dead. They saw him crucified. They saw the gush of water and blood from his side. They had the testimony of the Roman centurions, who were very good at killing. They had taken his body down and buried him. From their view, in their paradigm, there was no answer for death.

2. **Verses 12 and 13 briefly describe the appearance of Jesus on the road to Emmaus. The disciples did not believe that account either. Why?**

Again, they were trapped by concepts and beliefs that did not allow an answer for death. Jesus could not possibly be alive.

3. **Verse 14 says, "He rebuked them for their unbelief and hardness of heart, because they didn't believe those who had seen him after he had risen." Was there an expectation that the disciples should have believed Mary Magdalene and others who saw Jesus on the road to Emmaus?**

Yes, and the expectation carries forward to our time. Jesus expects us to believe the eye-witness accounts of the many people who saw him raised from the dead.

John 20:24-31

>²⁴But Thomas, one of the twelve, called Didymus, wasn't with them when Jesus came. ²⁵The other disciples therefore said to him, "We have seen the Lord!"

>But he said to them, "Unless I see in his hands the print of the nails, and put my hand into his side, I will not believe."

^{26}After eight days again his disciples were inside, and Thomas was with them. Jesus came, the doors being locked, and stood in the midst, and said, "Peace be to you." ^{27}Then he said to Thomas, "Reach here your finger, and see my hands. Reach here your hand, and put it into my side. Don't be unbelieving, but believing."

^{28}Thomas answered him, "My Lord and my God!"

^{29}Jesus said to him, "Because you have seen me,[114] you have believed. Blessed are those who have not seen, and have believed."

^{30}Therefore Jesus did many other signs in the presence of his disciples, which are not written in this book; ^{31}but these are written, that you may believe that Jesus is the Christ, the Son of God, and that believing you may have life in his name.

Jesus told Thomas that the people who believe the eye-witness accounts of the resurrection are blessed.

4. Why did Mark put these stories of disbelief immediately before verse 16?

Verses 10 and 11 describe the hardness of heart and disbelief of the disciples in relation to the message of Mary Magdalene. In verses 12 and 13, two disciples came from Emmaus with a message that they saw Jesus alive. The other disciples did not believe the message. Verse 14 describes Jesus appearing to them and rebuking them for their hardness of heart and disbelief. Verse 15 is the command to take the message to the world. Verse 16 declares that the people who believe the message and are baptized will be saved. The people who disbelieve the message will be condemned. Jesus is making the same point he did in the story of Thomas in John 20. The people who believe the message without seeing Jesus personally will be saved.

5. Jesus said, "He who believes and is baptized will be saved." Is baptism required for salvation?

---

[114]   20:29 TR adds "Thomas."

(Note: This is one of the most debated questions in church history. Both the form, candidate, and function of baptism have been debated endlessly. For those who need a better understanding of the background of this debate, a brief survey of arguments is included in Appendix A: Various Beliefs About Baptism. The teacher or small-group leader should be familiar with his or her beliefs on this topic and be able to guide the discussion and present relevant information. Please avoid any kind of argument. This topic has been argued endlessly by well-intentioned Christians for thousands of years.)

6. Do verses 17 and 18 teach that every believer will do every sign or only some believers will do some signs?

¹⁷These signs will accompany those who believe: in my name they will cast out demons; they will speak with new languages; ¹⁸they will take up serpents; and if they drink any deadly thing, it will in no way hurt them; they will lay hands on the sick, and they will recover."

If this passage is saying, "All of these signs will accompany every believer who believes," then our existence and identity as believers depends upon finding some demon-possessed people and practicing exorcism.

If it is saying, "Believers in general will do these things," then Jesus' prediction already came true.

> Cast out demons (Acts 5:16, 16:16-18)
> Speak with new languages (Acts 2:1-11, Acts 10:44-46, 1 Corinthians 14)
> Take up serpents (Acts 28:3-6)
> Drink any deadly thing; it will in no way hurt them
> Lay hands on the sick, and they will recover (Acts 3:6-8, 5:15-16, 9:36-43)

On one side of this issue are those who maintain that every believer today must do at least one of these signs to be a Christian. On the other side are those who maintain that these signs were done in the first century and no one today can do such things. The vast majority of Christians are in the middle and believe God still works miracles today when needed. Miraculous signs should never be a test of fellowship or authenticity.

7.   Do verses 19-20 make a better ending to Mark than verse 8?

Most people would agree that Jesus being received into heaven to sit at the right hand of God is a far better ending. It concludes the theme of the true identity of Jesus and the fulfillment of messianic prophecies.

The book of Acts picks from this point and continues the story of the early church. This is the story where the Holy Spirit is poured out on the early believers and empowers them to preach the Gospel to all nations.

Appendix A:
Various Beliefs About Baptism

The questions surrounding baptism have divided the church for millennia. Is baptism required for salvation? Is baptism only for church membership? Can babies legitimately believe and be baptized, or should baptism be put off until a person is able to choose? Is sprinkling water on a person valid baptism, or does a candidate have to be immersed in water?

FORM, CANDIDACY, AND FUNCTION

The proper form of baptism has been debated since the second century (and probably the first century). Some maintain that the only valid form of baptism is immersion of the whole person under water. Others accept sprinkling or pouring water on the candidate as valid forms of baptism. Still, others reject water all together and maintain that baptism is only by the Holy Spirit.

The proper candidate for baptism is also a major topic for argument and division. Some churches baptize infants and others refuse to baptize a person until they are old enough to believe and choose their own path.

The function of baptism is a core issue because it involves fundamental questions of salvation theology. Some believe that baptism is how and when a person becomes a Christian. These people maintain that baptism is the moment sin (guilt) is washed away. At that moment, the person becomes a Christian and the Holy Spirit comes to dwell in them. Others teach that salvation is by faith alone and baptism is an outward sign of an inward condition. These people teach that after a person is saved by believing in Jesus as their personal Lord and Savior, they are candidates for baptism. Many of these people also teach that baptism is for church membership rather than salvation.

FORM

Form refers to whether sprinkling, pouring, or immersion is the proper and acceptable way to be baptized.

Proponents of immersion argue that the practice of the first-century church was to immerse the candidate completely under water. They maintain the Greek word for baptism means "immerse." They cite Romans 6 as the reason to use immersion as the only valid form of baptism.

<u>Romans 6:3-4</u>

[3]Or don't you know that all we who were baptized into Christ Jesus were baptized into his death? [4]We were buried therefore with him through baptism to death, that just like Christ was raised from the dead through the glory of the Father, so we also might walk in newness of life.

Proponents of immersion maintain that baptism is a reenactment of the death, burial, and resurrection of Christ. They claim that the apostle Paul taught that those who are baptized share in the death, burial, and resurrection of Jesus. The sinner is put to death in repentance, buried in water, and raised to walk a new life of righteousness as a Christian.

Proponents of sprinkling and pouring as valid forms of baptism usually do not exclude immersion, but many proponents of immersion exclude sprinkling and pouring.

The vast majority of churches today teach that sprinkling water (or sometimes pouring water) on the candidate is just as valid as immersion. In many cases, the acceptance of sprinkling is motivated by a belief that infants can or should be baptized. Since it is impractical to immerse infants, sprinkling becomes an accepted form of baptism.

CANDIDATE

Who is a proper candidate for baptism? Are babies legitimate candidates for baptism, or does a person have to be old enough to believe and repent and choose Christ? Many churches practice infant baptism while a number of other churches or denominations practice only adult baptism.

A large part of Christendom teaches that baptism is a sacrament and a prerequisite for being an accepted member of a specific denomination. People say, "I was baptized a Catholic" or, "I was baptized a Lutheran" meaning they joined that denomination, usually as an infant. There is often an associated belief that in baptism, the candidate becomes a Christian and is saved. To these people, baptizing a baby as soon as possible is essential. Since it is not practical to immerse babies, sprinkling became the accepted form of baptism. Of course, most of these churches accept immersion as a valid form of baptism for adults, but it is rarely practiced.

Other churches maintain that baptism is in response to a believing faith in Jesus and, therefore, a candidate for baptism must be old enough to believe in Jesus. These churches may have some type of dedication ceremony for babies but put off the actual baptism until the age of ten or twelve.

FUNCTION

What is baptism for? Do you become a Christian when you are baptized? Does baptism wash away your sins? Do you become a member of the church when you are baptized? Do you receive the Holy Spirit when you are baptized? These questions about the function of baptism have done more to divide the church than any other topic.

Some believe baptism is a sacrament of the church and is essential for salvation and church membership.

Some reject the idea that baptism has anything to do with salvation. They believe baptism is an outward sign of an inward condition and separate from salvation. They reject a "works-based salvation," claiming that salvation is through "faith alone."

Ephesians 2:8-9

> [8]for by grace you have been saved through faith, and that not of yourselves; it is the gift of God, [9]not of works, that no one would boast.

This position interprets the works mentioned in Ephesians 2:9 as any religious activity required for salvation. Therefore, they reason, baptism cannot be required for salvation because it would be a work that makes us worthy of God's grace and nothing can make us worthy.

Christians who assert that baptism is an outward sign of an inward condition find additional support in John 3.

John 3:14-18

> [14]As Moses lifted up the serpent in the wilderness, even so must the Son of Man be lifted up, [15]that whoever believes in him should not perish, but have eternal life. [16]For God so loved the world, that he gave his one and only Son, that whoever believes in him should not perish, but have eternal life. [17]For God didn't send his Son into the world to judge the world, but that the world should be saved through him. [18]He who believes in him is not judged. He who doesn't believe has been judged already, because he has not believed in the name of the one and only Son of God.

Clearly, Jesus taught that salvation is through belief. This faith-only position defines belief as something that occurs internally and baptism is not part of believing; it is a sign or expression of belief.

Luke 23:39-43

> [39]One of the criminals who was hanged insulted him, saying, "If you are the Christ, save yourself and us!"

[40]But the other answered, and rebuking him said, "Don't you even fear God, seeing you are under the same condemnation? [41]And we indeed justly, for we receive the due reward for our deeds, but this man has done nothing wrong." [42]He said to Jesus, "Lord, remember me when you come into your kingdom."

[43]Jesus said to him, "Assuredly I tell you, today you will be with me in Paradise."

Proponents of faith-only salvation claim this passage clearly teaches that the thief on the cross believed in Jesus and accepted him as Lord and was saved for his faith without being baptized.

Romans 1:16-17

[16]For I am not ashamed of the Good News of Christ, for it is the power of God for salvation for everyone who believes; for the Jew first, and also for the Greek. [17]For in it is revealed God's righteousness from faith to faith. As it is written, "But the righteous shall live by faith."[115]

Many other passages are used to support the belief that salvation is by faith alone and baptism is done after a saving faith is achieved. For these Christians, baptism is generally for church membership and done "as an outward sign of an inward condition." It is practiced as a fulfillment of the commands to be baptized but not associated with salvation.

Other Christians maintain that baptism is part of believing and faith. They argue that believing is a process that starts with hearing the message about Jesus and continues until conviction is attained. They see baptism as the point at which a person's saving belief is complete. They claim that Mark 16:15-16 clearly demonstrates that baptism is part of belief.

---

[115] 1·17 Habakkuk 2:4

Mark 16:15-16

[15]He said to them, "Go into all the world, and preach the Good News to the whole creation. [16]He who believes and is baptized will be saved; but he who disbelieves will be condemned.

They assert that baptism is how a person becomes a Christian. In Acts 2:38-39, the apostle Peter commanded the people who had come to believe to "repent and be baptized for the forgiveness of their sins."

Acts 2:38-39

[38]Peter said to them, "Repent, and be baptized, every one of you, in the name of Jesus Christ for the forgiveness of sins, and you will receive the gift of the Holy Spirit. [39]For the promise is to you, and to your children, and to all who are far off, even as many as the Lord our God will call to himself."

Acts 22:14-16

[14]He said, 'The God of our fathers has appointed you to know his will, and to see the Righteous One, and to hear a voice from his mouth. [15]For you will be a witness for him to all men of what you have seen and heard. [16]Now why do you wait? Arise, be baptized, and wash away your sins, calling on the name of the Lord.'

1 Peter 3:21-22

[21]This is a symbol of baptism, which now saves you—not the putting away of the filth of the flesh, but the answer of a good conscience toward God, through the resurrection of Jesus Christ, [22]who is at the right hand of God, having gone into heaven, angels and authorities and powers being made subject to him.

John 3:1-8

[1]Now there was a man of the Pharisees named Nicodemus, a ruler of the Jews. [2]The same came to him by night, and said to him, "Rabbi,

we know that you are a teacher come from God, for no one can do these signs that you do, unless God is with him."

[3]Jesus answered him, "Most certainly, I tell you, unless one is born anew,[116] he can't see the kingdom of God."

[4]Nicodemus said to him, "How can a man be born when he is old? Can he enter a second time into his mother's womb, and be born?"

[5]Jesus answered, "Most certainly I tell you, unless one is born of water and spirit, he can't enter into the kingdom of God! [6]That which is born of the flesh is flesh. That which is born of the Spirit is spirit. [7]Don't marvel that I said to you, 'You must be born anew.' [8]The wind[117] blows where it wants to, and you hear its sound, but don't know where it comes from and where it is going. So is everyone who is born of the Spirit."

The people who argue that the function of baptism is salvation, forgiveness of sins, reception of the Holy Spirit, and church membership do not reject the proposition that we are saved by grace through faith and not by works. Passages of scripture that say Christians are not saved by works refers to works of the Jewish law. This position claims that saving belief does, in fact, act.

James 2:14-19

[14]What good is it, my brothers, if a man says he has faith, but has no works? Can faith save him? [15]And if a brother or sister is naked and in lack of daily food, [16]and one of you tells them, "Go in peace, be warmed and filled"; and yet you didn't give them the things the body needs, what good is it? [17]Even so faith, if it has no works, is dead in itself. [18]Yes, a man will say, "You have faith, and I have works."

---

[116] 3:3 The word translated "anew" here and in John 3:7 (anothen) also means "again" and "from above".

[117] 3:8 The same Greek word (pneuma) means wind, breath, and spirit.

Show me your faith without works, and I by my works will show you my faith.

[19]You believe that God is one. You do well. The demons also believe, and shudder.

The demons believe that there is a God and that Jesus is the Son of God, but just believing those facts does not save them because it produces no change in their behavior. Saving faith produces actions and changes in the person who believes.

The conclusion is that many honest, sincere, faithful people disagree on the form, candidacy, and function of baptism. The question is, will God actually say to someone on Judgment Day, "I'm sorry, George, you were sprinkled as an infant, and I only accept full-body immersion of adults, so even though you lived an amazingly faithful life, you will spend eternity in hell." Each person has to find their own opinion and belief in this topic.